Knitting, Tatting and Nervous Breakdowns

ALISON BRYSON

Knitting, Tatting and Nervous Breakdowns

First published in Australia by Alison Bryson 2020

 A catalogue record for this book is available from the National Library of Australia

ISBN: 978-0-6489465-0-2 (pbk)
ISBN: 978-0-6489465-1-9 (ebk)

Typesetting and design by Publicious Book Publishing
Published in collaboration with Publicious Book Publishing
www.publicious.com.au

This book is dedicated to those
who care for others.

CONTENTS

CHAPTER 1

Me

I was raised in a village. The type of village where generations of families went to the same school. Where people spoke to each other when they met in the street. Where vigilant villagers watched me cross the busy main road alone as a small child, before reassuring my parents I was capable.

Home was in the lands between the Scottish capital and the border with England, an area renowned for its historic lawlessness—its strong, fearless families who fought each other but then banded together to fight the southern enemy. An area where tradition was respected. Each year, the past revisited. The routes of ancestors were retraced by mounted cavalcades, inspecting the boundaries, checking for marauders and ensuring no encroachment. Their safe return was greeted by the townsfolk with cheers and jubilation—a celebration of that which had gone before.

Our village had a school, a magnificent red sandstone kirk and three pubs. There were small shops, a café and two church halls. Old men gathered on a bench, by the war memorial in the square, to while away the time. A bus service ran to other local villages and towns and up to the capital. The clock, in its imposing tower overlooking the square, chimed every hour. It was the heartbeat of the village.

There was Mum, Dad, me and my younger sister. And there were my uncles (Mum's younger twin brothers, who looked nothing alike but shared the same quick wit and devilish sense of humour) and both sets of grandparents. Although Dad was an only child, many of his cousins and their families lived in the village. And in the villages and towns beyond there were great-aunts, great-uncles and second cousins. There was family all around.

1

My earliest memories of my maternal grandparents involved wool. Grandpa worked in a mill and made rugs in his spare time; Gran knitted and crocheted. I used to help them with hanks of wool that needed to be wound into balls—holding my arms out shoulder-width apart with the hank looped over them, moving my arms in rhythm from side to side so that the wool slid off easily. My paternal grandparents lived in a house built in the mid-18th century, which had a large sloping back garden. Grandpa looked after the vegetables, while Gran cared for the fruit. My sister and I used to crawl into the hedge to gather windfallen plums before running down the garden to share our haul.

I was tall for my age, slim and a bit of a tomboy, a bit of a scrapper. Told never to make the first move, I would defend myself vigorously if needed. I loved running around, walking our dog and riding my scooter. I adored my scooter. I would whizz along the pavement, careen down hills and terrorise the villagers with my speed. Mum nicknamed me 'Scoot', although this was probably more to cover up her enduring inability to call me by my correct name. She starts off with 'Ali', morphs into my sister's name, and ends with 'who are you?' I was always on the go. My younger uncle nicknamed me 'lucky legs', as in 'you're lucky they hold you up', and together we joked, laughed and teased each other. I was my older uncle's shadow until he married and left the village. I thought of the passenger seat in his car as 'my seat' because I was in it so often. When I was upset because he was moving away, he knew he'd find me in his car. He reassured me there that he would forever be my uncle. My younger uncle married too and gained three stepchildren. I was thrilled to gain 'big' cousins! With three younger cousins joining us, we were a tight-knit band of six adults and eight children.

When my maternal grandpa died, we moved to live with Gran in the Victorian home she had been left by a relative. For a few years we were a group of five with two dogs. Gran was the person I went to if I couldn't sleep; she'd move over to cuddle me in her bed. Gran was the person who reassured me, when I was afraid because kids at school spoke of the world ending, that her school friends had spoken about this, too. And yet we were all still here. And Gran was the person who joined the local athletics club with me when I was too shy to go on my own. She loved helping with the younger kids and keeping fit. Growing up I felt secure in the love of my family and the knowledge that I always had someone other than my parents to turn to. As my sister and I grew older, Gran moved out to a small cottage, a short walk away, although she still spent a lot of time with us.

Holidays were wonderful, spent at the beach in our family caravan. Two weeks with Mum and Dad and other times with Gran and the younger grandchildren—a happy time of paddling, exploring rock pools and no socks. My sister and I also stayed on a hill-sheep farm where our 'aunt' lived. She was Mum's older cousin, whose hopes for marriage had been dashed by her guardian uncle, who had deemed her admirer unsuitable. She had become a nanny to a family with ten children. We loved staying with her, watching the farmer and his sons tend the sheep and work their dogs, feeding the goats and collecting eggs.

It was a simple, blissfully happy childhood. Although we probably didn't have much money and my sister and I wore hand-me-down clothes, we wanted for nothing. Mum, Dad and Gran made sure of that. Dad worked shifts as a delivery driver and Mum worked two part-time jobs, as well as being heavily involved in community activities, while Gran kept the house running. We regularly visited family, walked our dogs through the countryside and went for Sunday drives in the car, always having a picnic. Birthdays were celebrated with skilfully made cakes (Gran's 'At the ballet' cake was a sight to behold, although the hedgehog with halved chocolate buttons for spines was my favourite!), Christmases with small presents and lots of food—mince pies, Christmas cake, yule log—and Hogmanay (31 December) with drink, black-bun (a brick-shaped, pastry-encased, rich, dense fruitcake) and family. Everything was homemade: knitted jumpers, some with pictures on them; jam (stored in a cupboard in the second bedroom) of all sorts—strawberry, raspberry (always runny), blackcurrant, bramble, rhubarb and ginger, rhubarb and orange, gooseberry, damson, greengage, apple jelly and plum jam. Soups, stews and steamed puddings were made in the pressure cooker and there were always tins filled with sponges, rock buns or shortbread. Occasionally the door to the under-stairs cupboard would open to reveal a rabbit or pheasant (usually brought by my uncle), hanging and ready to be skinned or plucked by Gran.

Visitors, the more spontaneous the better, were always welcomed with tea, sandwiches and cakes. We would sit in a circle in the living room, listening as stories were recounted, punctuated with laughter, teasing and fun. And with love. The latest news from a great-aunt, her recent attempt to move to a secretarial career thwarted at the interview when she couldn't put paper in the typewriter. The Friday-night conversations of my uncle and the local characters in their 'regular'. The observations of a cycling great-uncle, who told us of the villages and people he passed on his journeys through the countryside. We would listen intently as the storyteller spoke, occasional comments from others thrown in. Then when the tale ended, another person would take the lead and start to share. No back-and-forth of questions and answers, but images woven from descriptions, emotions stirred from revelations, memories created.

I liked school. I had learned to read before starting school and was thrilled when Mum and her friend (and her two children of the same age) took us all to join the village library. It was something I had asked to do. As I looked around at all the books, I thought I was in heaven. Getting my own library ticket, borrowing books and learning new words was so exciting. I particularly liked the word 'hullabaloo' and was pleased when I could pronounce it. My love of reading has continued. It doesn't matter whether it's books, newspapers or adverts on the tube, if there are words, I have to read them.

I had a best friend. Her family lived in the village Gran, Grandpa, Mum and my uncles had lived in—a tiny one-street village, two miles away, with house names like Pumpkin Cottage and Thistle Cottage. She liked books too and we talked about the Famous Five and Nancy Drew. We were in the Brownies together, and we played in the woods by the river and cycled between our two villages. When she moved back to the capital, I felt bereft. Even though we kept in touch, I really missed her.

We were brought up to treat everyone the same and as we would like to be treated. Mum used to say we were 'all Jock Tamson's bairns' (children). I never knew who Jock was, but I understood it didn't matter what colour, age or religion we were. We were all people. We had a clear sense of right and wrong, probably honed by Mum's brilliant yet cruel punishment for misdemeanours (used to great effect after one scooter incident!). She made us sit and watch a clock. No reading or playing. Just sitting, staring at the hands of the clock as they moved slowly round. In some ways it was a strict upbringing. If our parents or Gran told us to do something, we did it. We lived within a framework of obeying rules, being polite and considerate, and observing Gran's little sayings and superstitions. No early morning singing for us, because 'sing before breakfast, cry before tea'. Weather forecasts were predicted by 'red sky at night, shepherd's delight . . . red sky in the morning, shepherd's warning'. Put on your jumper inside out? You had to wear it like that all day, otherwise bad luck would befall you!

While I loved being with my family, I was happy with my own company, too. I didn't need conversation or others around me; I was perfectly content to read, walk or listen to music. Generally, I was an easy-going person although I had a temper. I didn't get angry readily, but when I did, look out! It was a standing joke that someone had to have a chocolate bar at the ready in case I got hungry. Hunger usually resulted in a loss of concentration, followed by a blow-up.

I was nosey (*curious* seems a kinder word but *nosey* is probably more appropriate). When I was small, I would ask Mum and her friends to stop conversations if I had to leave the room, because I didn't want to miss what they were saying. As I grew older, I could be quite contrary (Mum worked out that the best way to get me to do something was to tell me *not* to do it) and I had a minor rebellious streak in my teens when I dyed my hair and swore a lot. (My rationale was that I didn't drink, smoke or do drugs, so things could have been a lot worse.)

Impatience was my middle name. When I decided on something, I had to get down to it immediately. However, I was also a bit of a butterfly, fluttering from one exciting thought or thing to the next, sometimes finding it hard to finish the task I was on. The next seemed more interesting or absorbing!

Community was important, and we played our part in village life. The annual festival week of sports, parades and dances was a special event in the calendar and we happily participated. After Brownies I joined the Guides. Mum was the leader and took us camping, joining other Guide companies on local farms or campsites. We each had a drawstring bag with a tin plate, mug and cutlery (Mum had a blob of pink nail varnish on her items to distinguish them) and a 'sitter' (a cushion with a waterproof bottom) for sitting round the campfire. When I was seventeen, I was a young leader at an international camp in Switzerland and was nicknamed 'Tiki' after the name of a sparkling water. The other guides recognised that although I was sometimes quiet, I could suddenly become bubbly and chatty. What I thought was a kidnapping in the middle of the night (we were marched out of camp into the woods by young men) turned out to be the initiation ceremony where my nickname was revealed. Mum thought they were spot-on in their assessment.

I loved running—really loved it. I'd joined the athletics club when I was nine and spent hours training with club members. Running through dark streets, wearing waterproofs when it rained, thumping up and down a particularly testing set of steps. Night after night I trained, running with older members, but keeping up. If they went out, I wanted to go too. Saturdays and Sundays were competitions. Middle distance, sprints, long- jump and relays in summer. Cross-country, my favourite, in winter. I adored running around our village, up and down farm tracks, over bridges, through woods. Nothing beat running through snow-covered woods. It was magical. I ignored sniffles and colds. I ran through them. I just wanted to run.

Until I couldn't. I had no energy. I was lethargic and had headaches. I couldn't concentrate and just wanted to stay in bed. The doctors did tests but couldn't tell what was wrong. I missed some school. My doctor said I had a virus, possibly Coxsackievirus. I had his sympathy, but there was nothing else he could give. Can you imagine how it felt? How lonely? It was the early 1980s; no one seemed to know what was wrong, and worse, I suspected people thought I was making it up. In the days before the internet and social media, there was no way to see if other people were similarly affected or find ways to help myself. My 'aunt' recommended a homeopath, and, in the absence of other help, we consulted him. He explained he was treating someone for similar symptoms and, with my agreement, passed on my details. They lived some distance away, so contact was by telephone. We compared histories, discussed symptoms and drew reassurance. At least I wasn't alone anymore.

I didn't know what I wanted to do after school, but I was advised to go to university. At the start of term, we drove to a city in the north and I embarked on a new adventure. I got to know people, joined clubs and societies, and became a member of the Students' Council. Despite this, I didn't like living in a city. I found it disconcerting because it was impersonal. People walked past without looking at one another, never mind saying hello or engaging in conversation. Although I became used to it, I never felt at home.

I wanted to make a difference. I found out that, while most students went home during the Christmas holidays, international students stayed in one large halls of residence. I loved organising events and so I started a Christmas programme with parties and entertainment. The local premier league football club offered free tickets to a match and a local bowling alley opened its doors for us. It was a fantastic opportunity to meet people from other cultures and backgrounds. And not just for me. We had our family Christmas there one year and for Hogmanay, two minibuses full of students turned up at home. The kitchen was taken over for traditional cooking while my older uncle wandered around offering everyone drinks.

University gave me other opportunities too, including the chance to live in West Germany for a year as part of my studies, teaching English to local schoolchildren. I found it interesting to explore another country, immerse myself in a different culture and observe the effects of reunification as 'Trabis' (the most common car in East Germany) began to be seen in Bavarian towns and villages. I was lucky to co-lead an exchange visit, taking a group of children back to my home area in Scotland, seeing it anew through their eyes.

University was also the place where I met my future husband. While I still didn't know what I wanted to do, he was already a postgraduate student with an academic career beckoning. I 'fell into' university administration. I pitched some ideas I had to a senior academic and landed a short-term contract, which led to a permanent position. While my then-boyfriend went to America after graduation, I stayed, working and living in the university. For three years we saw each other during holidays, when I would fly over, and we would explore North America. We wrote to each other, cards and letters regularly crossing the Atlantic. Correspondence deepened our relationship as we shared our innermost thoughts and wishes. We married after his return to a full-time academic position in Wales and I joined the medical school of a nearby university. For the next six years I worked with academics and doctors, managing a team to enrol students, organise their clinical placements, arrange exams and celebrate their graduation. My husband and I both worked hard. We had a similar work ethic. We enjoyed visits to our families and holidays abroad, which often coincided with conferences my husband attended.

The hard work resulted in a higher position for my husband in a new medical school in the south of England. Finding employment in a different part of the country was daunting, but something told me to look for a job involving exams. Coincidentally, the United Kingdom's medical regulator was seeking someone to manage a new assessment centre. International junior doctors, who wanted to work in the country, would have their clinical skills examined there. At the interview I was awed by the hiring manager—a no-nonsense woman with high expectations, who seemed to make things happen. To my delight, I was successful! I started this challenging role, leading a small team to run exams in a dedicated suite. We worked with doctors who created and assessed the multiple scenarios each candidate undertook (covering medicine, surgery, child health, psychiatry, obstetrics and gynaecology and other specialties) and with actors who played the parts of patients. This was a high-stakes exam, and I was passionate about ensuring the best experience for our candidates. We became internationally recognised, and I regularly hosted visitors from across the world, explaining our work.

When, after six years, the decision was taken to move the centre to a northern location, I sought a new job closer to our home. This time, I decided to look for a role that wouldn't change; one that would always be there. Another coincidence: A nearby local authority was looking for a manager for the registration service of births, deaths and marriages. Soon I was overseeing three managers and four offices of registration staff across a large county. I was based in a town on my own. My new managers wanted to make sure I didn't appear to favour one office over another. As it was used for birth and death registrations two days each week, I had to find alternative accommodation on those days. I felt isolated. I saw no one when I was there. The only 'contact' I had with the outside world was each Monday around 2 pm, when a local shopper tied up their dog outside. The dog clearly didn't like being left on its own and barked continually to let everyone know. This became the highlight of my working day.

CHAPTER 2

September 2010 – When It Happened

It seemed to start on that Friday morning with funerals. Well, funeral celebrants anyway. I'd been back at work for four days after a week-long holiday, but I didn't feel refreshed after the break. I felt tired and drained, but strangely, I was buzzing inside. While on holiday, I'd had these incredibly black, doom-filled feelings. They almost consumed me—made me feel sick. I'd be drifting on a rubber ring in the pool, seemingly without a care in the world, trying to suppress these feelings without knowing what was happening or why.

That Friday I walked up the hill to work, skirting the large houses in the crescent, thinking about the recruitment event for funeral celebrants. I was used to recruiting staff, though mainly clerical or technical staff. Still, the organisation of the event was similar: determine the activity and hold interviews. We'd decided to ask to candidates to prepare a eulogy in advance, deliver it in front of everyone, then hold individual interviews. Tick, all done. Book a large room for the eulogy delivery, a waiting room and smaller rooms for interviews. Tick, all done. Although not all the rooms were ideal, some weren't available for specific periods during the day. We would short-list applicants, invite them and give them necessary details. Tick. They had all confirmed their attendance. Finalise the timetable . . . not done. It needed to be. It shouldn't have been difficult to decide the order of eulogy presentations and interview times. Somehow my brain was taking its time to engage in the task. Every thought seemed to be slow, despite my pace, as I tackled the hill.

I'd put off organising the event, which was unusual. I loved organising things and had arranged functions, dinners and events involving hundreds of people. Why was this a problem? As I rounded a

9

bend, I suddenly felt my mind speed up—not just a little. The internal machinations of my brain took off at warp speed: do this, say that, explain to my boss. As if the possibility of failure had snapped my mind, now it was working at manic speed. As I walked, thoughts slammed into my head, each thought taking me closer to my goal. Hours later I had spoken to my manager, discussed my concerns, proposed a solution, and I was leaving work. Still no timetable. Time and again I'd tried, but the screen had remained blank. Frowning furiously, I'd started, then stopped, then started again. All the time, thoughts were running through my head: *How will I get this done? Have I too many candidates? Why is this so difficult? I don't know what I'm doing.*

That night, I blurted out my difficulties to my husband. He explained what he would do, but rather than listen, I ran to open my laptop to take notes. It all seemed so easy when he spoke, but I was confused. I asked questions to recap the points he made. From his facial expressions, I was getting things wrong. It seemed that I listened, understood, but then something changed all the words in my head. They became jumbled. I couldn't think straight. All the time thoughts were banging inside my head: *You've got to get this done. It's so easy, what's wrong with you? How useless are you?*

I collapsed into bed that evening, reassured that I had the whole weekend to get it right. I'd get it done. I just needed to rest. As usual, I fell asleep easily. I loved sleep and slept through thunderstorms, heavy rain and high winds. At 3.30 am I was wide awake. I bolted from the bedroom, put on the light and went downstairs, trying not to wake my husband. I pulled open the laptop and tried to log on. It wasn't responding quickly enough. I paced the room, went upstairs again, looked out on to the street below. Back downstairs, I tried to log on again. Eventually a Word document opened. I stared at it, but no inspiration came. It remained blank. My husband asked what I was doing. I told him I was trying to work, but he suggested I come back to bed. I looked at the screen again. Nothing. Still blank. I closed the lid and was led upstairs to bed. Sleep must have come, because before I knew it my alarm was going off.

Even though it was the weekend, my husband was going to work. It was the start of a new academic year and he would be busy, welcoming students, giving introductory lectures and attending events. I knew that the early weeks of term would be hard on him—a heavy teaching load, anatomy practicals, the pressure of setting expectations and creating the right environment for new students. He'd be gone all day, so I could work on the timetable. I sat down and recapped what needed to be done. Nothing was coming to me. 'Funeral Celebrant Interviews' stared back at me. I started to panic; why couldn't I do this? What was happening? I made a cup of tea and sat staring at the screen. Holding my arms tight around me, I started to rock. I needed to move. I couldn't stay still. My arms wound tighter; I became hot and had a sudden urge to wet myself. My head was spinning. *I have to do this* whirled into my head. *I don't know what I'm doing* was the reply. My husband would make everything all right, I thought. I rang him and explained briefly that I still hadn't planned the timetable. Patiently he explained again what I should do. A calmness descended over me. Everything became clear. It was simple. The same blank page continued to stare at me.

By early afternoon, nothing had changed. I'd made another cup of tea and tried to settle down, but I had to keep moving. I decided a colleague might be able to help and so I gathered my things. With a new sense of energy, I drove off in my little car to the registration office, where she was conducting ceremonies. *My colleague will make everything all right*, I thought. *She'll know what to do.*

As I approached, a wedding party came out. They looked at me, all seeming to stare. I found my colleague clearing the ceremony room and explained my predicament. She suggested we could work things out on Monday morning. I was aware I was talking non-stop, not listening. She tried to reassure me we had time and arranged to meet me, so I drove home. I needed to try again, so I sat at the kitchen table looking at the same words: Funeral Celebrant Interviews. When my husband came home, he found me there. I was like a broken record, telling him that I didn't know what to do. I was getting more and more frustrated. When we went to bed, I was still harping on about funeral celebrants.

The timetable wasn't complete by Sunday afternoon. We had gone to the beach, but the wind hadn't blown any of the cobwebs in my head away. Back home, my husband suggested I clear out my work bag. I couldn't make sense of it. Which papers did I need to keep? What could be thrown away? I felt completely drained. I couldn't stop talking. I talked and talked until my husband asked for just five minutes of quiet.

I was silent for a few heartbeats. Then my mouth opened, and I started to talk about funeral celebrant interviews. My husband was frustrated and again asked me to be quiet. Why couldn't I stop talking? I looked at the meal I was picking at. I had no appetite. I whirled out of the room and went upstairs with no real purpose. My husband found me in our bedroom, arms wrapped tightly around me. 'I don't know what's happening', I said. 'I don't know who I am anymore.'

That was so unfamiliar. I'd always had my own sense of identity. I'd always known who I was. I was me. A forty-one-year-old, right-handed (but curiously left-footed) woman, who always led with my left leg when I stepped off a pavement. I was principled and determined. I was tongue-tied (not that I couldn't talk) as my tongue was attached to the bottom of my mouth. It meant I couldn't whistle and had to concentrate hard to pronounce words with the letters *r* and *l* in them. Irony: I married a man whose name contains two r's and two l's.

I didn't like heights but loved tomatoes. Although I'd held leadership roles, I was probably more comfortable in a second-in-command type role (possibly as a result of being my uncle's little shadow). I had a natural smile that people commented on (embarrassing when a passer-by stopped to ask me to smile again; I'm not good at doing things on command, and he left disappointed by my rictus grin) and a caring nature, putting others first.

I was capable. I made sure the girls in my care were OK when our international camp had to be evacuated due to flooding, meaning the leaders didn't need to worry. And I was calm. A doctor friend once said she wanted me with her in an emergency, after watching as I co-ordinated an ambulance for a sick relative, while continuing to talk and reassure them that they would be OK.

I enjoyed rock music and country and western (the Friday night dance of our village's festival was a favourite, as people wearing Stetsons and checked shirts arrived while 1970s country and western classics blared) and, despite my age, had a real love of soft toys. I'm amazed material and stuffing can make toys full of character and life.

Most of all, I knew I was me. Mum had worked in community education and when I was small, she told me about a training session where the group had been asked, as an icebreaker, 'Who are you?' One by one they said they were someone's wife, husband, mother, father, daughter, son, and so on. Until Mum. She said, 'I'm me'. I loved hearing this story. I was proud that Mum saw herself as an individual in her own right. As I got older, I asked her to tell me it again and again. Mum made sure I grew up knowing I was an individual too. That before I was defined as someone's daughter, sister, granddaughter, niece or cousin, I was me: Alison.

So, standing in our bedroom, my husband holding me by the upper arms, me not knowing who I was or what was happening, was devastating and frightening. I began to have thoughts about hurting myself. Taking tablets. Using a knife. Looking back, I know exactly what I should have done—sought help. But that moment, in that situation, in that room with my husband, I didn't know anything. I was aware my mind was working overtime. I put on a CD of ocean waves, lay on the sofa and tried to relax. My mind continued to race. When one thought came into my head, it was followed immediately by another and another.

The next morning, I drove to the most northerly of the offices. Arriving early, I parked and called Mum. My dad had been ill, and I wanted to know how he was, but I also needed to tell her that I didn't know what was happening to me. That, on the drive over, I'd thought about driving into a tree. She listened calmly, reassured me that Dad was fine and told me if it wasn't for her regular volunteer shift at the local court coffee bar that morning, she would drive to be with me. She said she would call my husband and speak to me later. She reassured me that everything would be all right and I should tell my manager how I was feeling.

After the office opened, I spoke to the colleague I'd seen at the weekend and explained I needed to speak to my manager. As more staff members arrived, I felt they were looking at me. I felt uneasy . . . uncertain. I wanted to hide. Coincidentally, my manager arrived for a meeting, and soon we were in a private office where I blurted out my difficulty with the recruitment event. I explained the situation, what I thought needed to be done and the consequences of taking this action. He reassured me that we had time to arrange it. Although I heard what he said, I didn't take any notice and continued to speak quickly, telling him of my struggles. My manager reminded me that we had discussed this before the weekend (had we?) and there was time to resolve the problems I had identified. My mind kept on whirring at top speed as I repeated what I'd said very quickly, barely drawing breath. My manager interjected. He was concerned about me. Thought I should go home. I protested. I had to arrange the timetable, there were problems and . . . again, he interrupted me. We were going in circles.

While my manager left to speak to my colleague, I tried to work out what I could do to organise the event. Maybe I could do this? Maybe that would work. Would this be better? My mind whirled and whipped. My manager and colleague both entered the room and explained that the event would be passed to two of my colleagues, so I could go home. I felt relief. I wouldn't have to think about this anymore. I assured them I was fine to drive, but I wanted to hand over information. My manager arranged for me to meet them at another office, so I filled my water bottle, grabbed my bag and headed off.

Although I had said I could drive, in truth I felt a bit erratic. Heavy on the brake, heavy on the accelerator. As I drove, I swigged regularly on my water bottle. Soon I was with my colleagues, explaining what had been organised so far. They listened, asked a few questions, but they seemed unconcerned about the task ahead. With reassurances that everything would be fine and I should go home, they walked me out. Waved me off. As the door closed, I stayed looking at it. I had a strange feeling that I wouldn't see them for some time.

I drove home, bombing through the country roads, keeping to my side of the road for the most part. Although maybe taking corners a little too wide? After one risky manoeuvre, I screeched to a halt in a farm entrance, took a long drink and told myself to be more careful. Drawing back on the road, I frantically checked my mirror. Had I left enough distance before the following car? Soon I was nearly home. I drove into a space by the small pond and managed to apply the handbrake before hitting the fence. I wanted to get inside quickly, so waved at my neighbour's husband rather than talking and unlocked the door.

I stood on the other side. What should I do now? I had to do something. I should be working. I texted my husband to tell him I was home and noticed an email had come in. I realised I didn't have to deal with it. There was relief as I switched off my work phone and put it away. I needed to keep moving. Hoovering would keep me occupied. I got the hoover but then looked at it as if it was a strange object. How did it work? Where was the on/off button? How did the attachments unclip? I pulled and pushed, hoping that something would happen, and

I could get underway. The machine roared to life and soon I was chasing it across the floor, like an owner with a large, untrained dog on a lead. I winced as I bashed the coffee table but didn't stop. I had to keep going. Forwards and backwards at high speed. Cursing at furniture in my way. Cringing at the loud bangs that ensued. As I switched it off, I was happy that I'd done something useful. I didn't seem to have done much damage. My phone rang and my husband explained that he and Mum had decided I should spend a few days in Scotland. Maybe I would feel better once I saw that Dad was OK.

A flight was booked for that evening, so now I had something else to do. I picked out a few clothes, got my toiletries together and packed a small bag. I couldn't sit still to watch television or read. I paced up and down the kitchen. I went out into the garden and walked up and down, came back in and paced to the living room. Back to the kitchen to look at the clock. I wanted to get on my way. I wanted to get on the plane. I wanted to be somewhere else.

I asked my husband to check what I'd packed when he got home. As we drove, he asked if I had eaten. I hadn't. I wasn't hungry, but I continued to drink water. He insisted that I eat some sweets. At departures he cuddled me closely before I walked to the plane. The short flight was uneventful, but I struggled to sit still. I jiggled my legs. Interlocked my fingers. Pulled them apart. Rubbed my hands down my thighs. Anything to keep moving. The magazine I bought went unread. Soon we were on our descent and I was walking towards Mum and Dad.

Mum enveloped me in a cuddle, pushed Dad towards me so I could see he was well and told me everything would be OK. I was glad to see them, glad to be cocooned in the car as we drove home. After about an hour I had to ask them to stop. I felt sick. Strange. I was never travel sick. Arriving home was like any other time though, a rush of welcoming, warm air followed by the aroma of baking. Although Mum wanted me to eat, I couldn't. I didn't feel hungry. They chatted to me, with Mum telling me about her stint at the court coffee bar and Dad talking about developments with the local Paths Group. It felt familiar, but I didn't feel like me. I was listening, even contributing occasionally, but I was distracted. Although I'd been relieved not to be at work the next day, now my head was filled with worry that I wasn't there.

The next couple of days passed as I walked with Dad, visited Gran and helped Mum as she cooked. My sister and I caught up, but I wasn't chatty or laughing the way I usually did. My mind seemed to have slowed slightly, but thoughts continued to swirl through my head. *You should be doing this . . . Why aren't you doing that? You're letting people down. What's happening to me?* On and on the thoughts circled around and around, without stopping.

That night Mum went out to a meeting and I called my husband. He asked how I was feeling. I didn't know. What was I going to do tomorrow? I didn't know. What was going to happen now? I didn't understand. He explained that I had left work, gone up to my parents, but for how long? What would happen now? I didn't know. I didn't know. I didn't know. My mind started whirling, thoughts slamming into me from left and right, buffeting me from side to side. I didn't know. I didn't know. I didn't know anything.

I told him I had to go, put down the phone and shoved my feet into my trainers, barely taking time to tie them. Opening the sitting room door, I told Dad as he glanced up from his newspaper that I was going to see Gran. Opening the large front door, I sprinted into the night, down the quiet street with the field on one side and houses on the other. Beneath the soft pools of the streetlights, I ran as if my life depended on it. I had to get away.

Even though I was running, I stopped to shut the gate, out of habit, I suppose. The waterside was so familiar to me. We'd walked our dogs there, played tennis and ball games, gone to the funfair there during festival week and, with the Guides, made campfires on the stony outcrops by the river. I knew where I was, and the familiarity of the place accompanied my every step. It didn't matter that it was dark, the only light that of the moon. I knew the width of the path, the little turn it took as it sloped gently down towards the small clump of trees to the right beyond the bench. The wild garlic filled my nose and reassured me about my progress. Darkness surrounded me. I continued running, as if I were being chased, until I left the path and went down the bank.

The river was running fast. Dad and I had watched it from the bridge earlier that day, swirling and frothing. I moved from the soft bank to the stones and felt the water fill my shoes. Cold but not breathtaking. I walked forward, feeling the stones beneath my feet, my trouser legs getting wet, billowing out with the water. As I went further, thoughts continued to slam into my head. Not gentle thoughts that emerged and bloomed but harsh, horrible thoughts that hurt. Like I was watching a PowerPoint presentation that wasn't in front of me, but in my head. *You don't know what you're doing*—BAM—the thought dropped from the top, then bounced up and down. *You're letting people down* barrelled in from the left, screeching to a halt as *You'll be found out* swept in from the right, almost like a blow to my head. *They think you're not doing a good job* dropped from the top again, leaving me reeling. *You don't know what you're doing* hit me again, this time from the left. Each new thought pounded into me before I was able to deal with the previous one. I just wanted it to stop. I wanted my head to stop hurting. I wanted to be taken away and not think anymore. I didn't know what to do, I didn't know what would happen next, I didn't know what was happening to me. I just wanted it to stop. The water was waist-high but still not too cold. My top was wet, and my clothes and shoes were feeling heavier. I was in the middle of the river, but the current wasn't picking me up. I sank down and immersed myself, hoping the water would take me and stop my thoughts. I put my head underwater but bobbed back up again. I hated water going up my nose, but I tried again and again. The thoughts were still hitting my head, from left and right, top and bottom. Why wouldn't they stop? Or slow down? Gradually I realised the river wasn't taking me away. There was nothing left for it but to pull myself up onto the bank, where I lay face down. I wanted to cry but no tears came.

I sobbed a little, becoming aware I was in a bed of nettles. As the stings became uncomfortable, I got to my knees and crawled up the bank. I stood as I reached the path and trudged back the way I'd come. Slowly. Dripping. Squelching. As I opened the large gate, I saw a figure under the streetlight walking down over the bridge—the first person I'd seen. It was my dad. He came over and asked what I was doing. Noticing that I was soaked through, he gathered me into his side as he walked me up the road. I said I'd put myself in the river. He held me tight and said that I'd run off so fast he couldn't see where I'd gone. Tying his shoes had held him up. He ushered me into the house and straight through to the bathroom, where he ran a bath. He told me to get in, clothes and all, while we waited for Mum to come home. As I lay in the water, the cold slowly left my clothes, replaced by a gentle warmth. But thoughts continued to pound my head.

CHAPTER 3

October 2010 – Incapable

The front door closed, and I heard a muffled conversation, while Dad told Mum what had happened. She came to the bathroom and cuddled me, ignoring that she was getting wet. She immediately said we needed help, and soon I was sitting by the phone, speaking to an operator from the 24-hour National Health Service medical assistance line. We were told to go to the local hospital where they'd be expecting us. There we were, sitting in an empty green waiting room, surrounded by posters about washing hands and clinical targets. Mum held my hand, but we didn't talk much. Thoughts still slammed into my head. *What's happening to me? How long will this take? I've got to get back to work.* When my name was called, I walked carefully and deliberately into the consulting room. The doctor was young and Asian. I wondered if he had taken the clinical exam I had been responsible for organising.

He asked why I was there and whether I smoked, drank, took recreational drugs or had any allergies. Despite everything, I remembered that I was allergic to an antibiotic, which brought me out in large red weals. Soon the doctor went to consult a senior colleague and came back with tablets, which I was to take before returning the next day to see a psychiatrist.

Next morning Mum told me to shower before we went back to the hospital. It seemed like everything was in slow motion, each action taking every possible piece of concentration I had. Turning off the shower required a supreme effort to co-ordinate the thought with the physical action. What to wear? I'd only brought a few clothes, but I knew appearance was important. The actors, who played depressed or suicidal patients in the clinical exam, dressed untidily, giving the impression they didn't care about themselves or how they looked. But I wasn't depressed. Was I? The patients in the exam scenarios were never happily married and living in a nice house.

The hospital waiting room was much busier, and I worried that people would know what I'd done and see that I was going off my head. Because that's how I felt. My thoughts were completely different to the ones I usually had. I asked Mum to come with me to see the doctor. I think I felt that I needed her to hear everything, but maybe I just didn't want to be alone. A tall female doctor asked the same history-taking questions as the doctor the previous night. I answered easily and was reassured that I could still remember the name of the antibiotic I was allergic to. Then suddenly, 'Why did you try to harm yourself last night?' I fumbled for words, but none came. Again, 'Why did you try to harm yourself last night?' I looked helplessly from the doctor to Mum, then back again. I muttered something about cuts at work and Dad being ill. 'You're not answering the question', the doctor said. I looked down as she repeated, 'Why did you try to harm yourself last night?' Still I had no answer and stared at my feet.

For some reason I couldn't tell her about the thoughts that had hurt my head—couldn't tell her that I wanted them to stop. That I didn't know what else to do. I felt scared when the doctor said, 'Alison, you're not answering my question', before leaving the room. Mum held my hand and tried to reassure me that I would be OK. When the doctor came back, she asked if Mum could look after me. If not, they were going to admit me to a psychiatric unit, although I didn't realise that at the time. Mum said she would look after me at home and the doctor then addressed me in gentler tones, telling me that I looked exhausted. I was. I wanted to sleep. I listened as she said she'd give me medication, not understanding what she said. She told me when to take the tablets and asked me to repeat what she'd said. I couldn't. She wrote everything down for Mum and told me not to worry. Then the doctor explained the Crisis Team attached to the local mental health service would contact me the next day. Leaving the consulting room, Mum took my arm to guide me along the corridor; I listened as she and Dad spoke, but all I wanted was to go to bed and sleep.

I don't remember much more about that day. While Dad went to the chemists, Mum put me to bed. I know I slept because in the odd moments I was awake, I was aware of the burning, sore sensation of nettle stings from the riverbank. The front of my body, my shins, thighs, stomach, chest, neck and chin felt as if they were on fire, even though Mum had dabbed me with calamine lotion. Somehow this physical pain felt good; I was feeling something. My head might be fuzzy. Inside I felt nothing, but my body was feeling heat and pain. The only other thing I remember was Mum leaning over, stroking my hair and face as I lay, looking up at her with eyes that struggled to stay open. 'You have beautiful eyes, Ali, just like your grandpa's, with lovely golden flecks in them.' Momentarily I felt moved, but tiredness descended and I fell back to sleep.

That night Mum called my husband. I heard her speak so I went downstairs to join her. I tugged at her arm as if I was a child. 'Have you told him what I did?' I asked. Mum brought over a stool and cuddled me close into her as I sat and haltingly told my husband what I'd done. It didn't seem like me saying the words. I can't remember his reply, but he said at least I had chosen something I couldn't do. On our last holiday he had tried patiently to encourage me to put my head under water, but I just couldn't. After talking for a few minutes, we said that we loved each other and put the phone down. While I was safe in the bosom of my family, I had told him this terrible thing and he was on his own, with no one to talk to.

Mum said she had decided to sleep in bed with me at night because she was worried I'd feel alone. In truth, she was probably more worried that I might try to harm myself again. She later told me that she and Dad had hidden the large front door key so that I couldn't leave the house at night, even if I wanted to.

The Crisis Team called the next day to arrange their first visit. Mum led me to the phone and sat me down to speak to them. It was a young woman, the sister of someone I had gone to school with. I worried she would tell people about the state I was in, but Mum reassured me that she had to keep her work confidential. I suppose I was embarrassed. I'd become a wreck who had to be led around the house and given medication. When I answered the door to her, I was wearing a pair of novelty slippers, hedgehogs I had long-ago named Horace and Herbert. It didn't occur to me that strangers might not appreciate my well-loved and much-repaired foot attire. We sat in the living room, Mum, me and the lady from the Crisis Team. How I was feeling? Very fuzzy in the head. What medication was I taking? Mum had to answer, as 'Here, take this, Ali' had become a familiar refrain and I had no idea. What were my plans for the next day? Plans. Somehow, I understood plans were important. What was I planning? No idea. I looked at Mum for encouragement and she explained she had to bake, so I would help.

The next day a male colleague visited. Again, Mum and I sat with him and talked. How was I feeling? No idea, really. Was I depressed? Me? I was happily married, had a loving family, a lovely home and a job I found challenging. How could I be depressed? Although I had considered my appearance before meeting the psychiatrist, it wasn't connected to depression. Was it? His question about whether I could be depressed took the wind out my sails. He then asked a series of standard questions about smoking, drinking and recreational drugs, all of which I'd covered before with other health professionals. Did I find enjoyment in the things I used to? Did I laugh as much? Look forward to things? With an embarrassed look to Mum, had I gone off sex? Was my appetite as good as normal? I sat, trying to think. I used to laugh. I enjoyed making other people laugh, but my husband had commented that I hadn't laughed so much lately. Maybe I was depressed. The Crisis Team member asked if I was relaxing and if I breathed using my diaphragm. He suggested we all take a deep breath and then told me no, I hadn't breathed correctly. I had raised my shoulders, indicating I used only the top part of my lungs, rather than enjoying a deep breath from my diaphragm. Who knew? A relaxation tape would help, he said, before asking about my plans for the next day. Plans! This time I was ready. I had plans. I was going to help Mum bake. Again. What was I going to make? Ah, maybe not so well planned after all. I had no idea but blurted out 'Shortbread'. Probably news to Mum, but she kindly didn't disagree!

My sister had plans. She planned to buy a flat-pack bookcase and so I joined her and Mum a few days later in a store I was familiar with. It had catalogues spread throughout and small blue pens to write down product codes on order forms. However, I found it hard to search through the catalogue. The heavy pages seemed resistant to turning. There were so many items to choose from. It was confusing. I tried to search the index but didn't make much headway. I couldn't find bookcases in either the laundry or children's toys sections. Mum and my sister found the item, ordered and paid, and we waited to collect it. When the item came, my sister tried to lift it, but it was heavy. I moved Mum out the way before she could try to lift it. Despite their objections, I was determined to carry it. I hadn't been able to do anything else. Didn't drive us over, couldn't find the item in the catalogue, wasn't sure what was going on, but I would carry the package, no matter how heavy. I wondered whether I needed to demonstrate my physical strength to compensate for my mind not working. Later, I watched as Mum and my sister put the bookcase together. It took a while (Mum has an electric drill and enthusiasm, but not necessarily furniture-putting-together skills) but soon I was helping my sister fill her bookcase.

Mum thought I should knit something. Both she and Gran were keen knitters, always with projects on the go. Mum loved knitting baby shawls and men's socks, while Gran liked to try new techniques from books she ordered. A few minutes after the suggestion, needles were in my hand and I was instructed to knit squares for blankets, to be given to those in need.

Although it was some time since I knitted (probably it had been last time I stayed with Mum and Dad), the needles felt familiar and comfortable in my hands. Soon I was casting on the required number of stitches for an undemanding pattern. Plain knitting, no increase or decrease in stitches. Still, I used a small piece of paper to jot down each completed row. We sat in contented silence with the television in the background. Mum was making a wall hanging, with a hessian-type material back and strips of old woollen jumpers threaded through. She had found a picture in a magazine—a tree by a beach—and needed shades of orange, gold and black to replicate it. I'd helped her choose the colours earlier. I'd stared up into the tall cupboard filled with worn-out jumpers with holes under the arms and other signs of wear and tear. Mum had assured me they were too good to throw out. Now they'd come in useful. The scale of Mum's project seemed daunting, as I turned my attention back to my knitted square and marked down another completed row.

Days later my younger uncle told us Gran had had a visitor. Nothing unusual, you might think. Two questions usually follow the announcement of a visitor. Not 'who?' and 'when?' But 'where?' and 'size?' Our family calls rodents 'visitors'. As if not saying the words *mouse* or *rat* makes the situation more palatable.

Indoors. Small. A mouse had run from underneath Gran's chair across the small channel of carpet before disappearing. Gran was a hoarder, but not in the horrible-plastic-bags-filled-with-God-knows-what-and-stale-food-everywhere type of hoarder. She just had lots of stuff. She was a child of the Depression; her mother had died in childbirth and her father had lost the family farm. Gran and her six brothers and sisters had been split up, with Gran put into service as a maid. She knew what it was to have nothing. Consequently, she kept everything. Her cottage was packed with furniture, antiques, books, magazines, wool and craft materials.

Mum was less than thrilled at the prospect of investigating the visitor, but we walked to Gran's. While Mum sat in the high-backed chair explaining our plans, I perched on a chair arm that peeked out from under clothes, newspapers and knitting patterns. I had to take care—everything might fall. Gran sat in her large, rose-coloured armchair, cocooned in its warmth. Next to her on the wall were family pictures; a photo of her late, lamented collie, Snap; and a little plaque with antique writing that read 'Today's the tomorrow you worried about yesterday and all is well'.

Mum and I began to hunt. Mum picked things up and handed them to me, to put somewhere else. We worked carefully. Moved things with caution. Found a hidden chair, filled with books and bags of wool. We reached Gran's spinning wheel, propped against a table. On top of it was a clock, some pictures and dishes with safety pins, drawing pins, picture hooks and nails. No sign of the visitor.

Gran was cold, so the heating was turned up. We picked our way to the corner of the room, moving one pile after another. A record player (covered with newspaper cuttings), a collection of 78 RPM records, a knitting machine, another pile of books, a knitting machine table. As Mum hoovered (all the time mindful of the piles of 'things' around us), we discussed our next plan of attack. Gran, obviously warmer and keen to be involved, took charge of directing operation-put-everything-back-where-you-found-it from her chair. I don't know how, but she told Mum the order to put things back and where exactly each item should be placed. Soon, it was like we hadn't been there. My uncle arrived to lay some traps and commented on a funny smell as he entered. We hadn't noticed anything. Traps set, we went for lunch. When we returned, there was a strange odour. I thought it seemed strongest near Gran, happily baking, but still with a shawl on. We searched around Gran's chair, moving things: letters (opened but still in their envelopes) in piles; stacks of magazines (all in date order) leaned up against chair legs; books in rows under the window; bags of wool and craft material. We drew another blank.

I left to go to a doctor's appointment. As I waited, I thought how strange it felt to be back. None of the doctors were familiar, although the health centre was. I explained to the doctor that I was visiting family, had been unwell, had gone to casualty and had regular visits from the Crisis Team. Mum had told me to ask for a doctor's certificate for work, so she wrote one and passed it to me. 'Acute anxiety' was the reason for absence. We discussed the medication I was taking, and I asked her to check my ears. Maybe I had river water in them, I thought. All was OK. As I got up to leave, she looked at me sadly and said, 'You've no idea what's happening to you, have you?' She was right. I didn't. I had no clue. She didn't tell me anything. No warnings or advice. Nothing.

At Gran's, I noticed another strong smell. Disinfectant! Mum was washing the unused hearth, my uncle tying up a black bag. Mission accomplished. Several visitors captured. One was found in the box that encased Gran's radiator pipes, by her armchair. Turning up the heating had cooked not only Gran but her visitors too! We congratulated ourselves on our success. As we left, I wondered if I might have a career in pest control. I obviously wouldn't be able to return to my management role.

Back home, Mum told me to send the certificate to my manager. I took some paper and an envelope from the drawer—then realised that I didn't know how to write a letter. What should I say? How could I explain what was happening? I stared at the paper before calling Mum for help. Gently she suggested I write her address and the date in the top right-hand corner. On the left-hand side, the name and address of my manager. I remembered his name and a vague address, but not the postcode. Mum searched on her laptop to find it.

What now? Mum suggested a brief message. A medical certificate was enclosed to cover one week's absence and I would be in touch, when I could. No need for anything more. She said my husband was in contact with my manager and would tell me if anything else was required. Carefully I wrote the name and address on the envelope.

Mum photocopied the letter and certificate, stuck on a stamp and asked Dad to walk to the post box. It would catch the evening collection.

The Crisis Team member visited again. I was determined to breathe properly and have suitable plans! Mum and I had agreed to make soup next day. I was still taking medication, but when he asked, I couldn't name it. He explained that the first nurse would return to review my medication and provide another prescription. He gave me a relaxation CD and information about sleeping. Apparently, it was best to get up at the same time each morning and not catnap during the day. He also gave me a small card titled 'Living Life to the Full . . . Helping You to Help Yourself.'[1] I hadn't felt like reading since becoming unwell, but this had short statements, so I started to read:

'The Rules of Assertion—I have the right to:

1. Respect myself—who I am and what I do.
2. Recognise my own needs as an individual.
3. Make clear 'I' statements about how I feel and what I think.
4. Allow myself to make mistakes.
5. Change my mind, if I choose.
6. Ask for 'thinking it over time'.
7. Allow myself to enjoy my successes.
8. Ask for what I want.
9. Recognise that I am not responsible for the behaviour of other adults.
10. Respect other people and expect the same in return.
11. Say I don't understand.
12. Deal with others without being dependent on them for approval'.

Immediately I had problems. 'Respect myself—who I am and what I do.' I didn't know who I was. What I'd become. I didn't recognise myself in this person who needed visits from the Crisis Team, who took medication. I decided to keep the card but not read or think about it again.

A routine developed. I'd wake at 7.30 am and go downstairs to the kitchen, to find Dad making a pot of tea. I'd ask if he slept well. Tell him if I'd heard him or Mum go downstairs in the night to the bathroom. The stairs creaked as they went. 'See, I'm not sleeping', I'd say. 'You've got to sleep, just let yourself', he'd reply, shaking his head.

I'd go to shower, slowly and deliberately, every movement requiring effort and attention. Ablutions completed, I'd return to the kitchen to find Mum making breakfast after visiting Gran and collecting newspapers. As we sat at the table, Mum would begin to read out news from the paper, while I took my medication.

Dad had collected my first prescription, but I walked to the chemists to get the second one. The chemists sat beneath the clock tower, and I anticipated the heavy resistance of the door. As I handed over the script, I mused that I was every druggie's dream, although I might not look it. An ideal target: anti-depressants, diazepam, temazepam—all the pams! I couldn't defend myself if there were addicts in the village who'd mug me for my jellies. I heard the assistant query who the prescription was for. There was me and one other customer. The chemist nodded towards me and the assistant apologised as she passed me the pills. She'd recognised me by my maiden name. My married name had confused her. I walked home and added my drugs to the kitchen drawer.

The female doctor who had seen me in casualty visited one day, not the Crisis Team as expected. Horrors! I swallowed as I showed her to the living room and got Mum for support. The visit was like the others. How was I feeling? Was I taking medication? Was I sleeping? What plans did I have for the next day? A walk with Dad and baking with Mum—oatcakes and sausage rolls. Hmm, my planning skills were getting better! I would also play the relaxation CD her colleague had brought. As she left, I said I had found her 'very scary' at the hospital but now thought she was quite nice. She laughed and said thank you. It was a small achievement. I'd dared to say what I thought.

I tried the relaxation CD, tensing different body parts, then releasing to feel the tension ease. I followed the instructions of a quietly spoken woman. Occasionally she shuffled papers, as if reading from a script. Mum joined me on the living room floor, as we lay tensing our arm, face, shoulder and neck muscles. Invariably I fell asleep, which I took to be a good sign. Obviously, I was relaxing! Probably, though, it was the medication I was taking.

Our daily routine continued with watching *Bargain Hunt* over lunch before Dad retired to watch a western (or have a snooze!) while Mum and I visited Gran, baked or knitted. We spoke to my husband each night, but he didn't talk about work. (I found out later this was under strict instruction from Mum.) We deliberately hadn't told Gran what I'd done. We didn't want to worry her. She seemed to sense something though. My sister said Gran had asked if Alison was taking drugs. I wasn't talking or behaving in my normal way. She was right. Just not in the way she thought.

Do you know what it's like not to recognise your own head? I think we all get used to our heads. I'll look around, seeing what I see. I'll think over conversations, reflect on what was said and what I should have said. I'll plan—things to do, places to go, people to see and, if I'm driving, the route I'll take. I'll remember things, silly things that are inconsequential—the surnames of students from a long time ago. Inevitably my thoughts will start with one thing and then divert to another and another. Before I know it, I'll be far away from my original thought. There's also what I like to think of as my mind wallpaper: music. It's always there. A song or tune I've heard that resonated. Moved me. Playing in the background to my thoughts. My own little musical accompaniment. Only now there was silence. Nothing. I had observational thoughts. That was all. I saw things. Nothing more. My thoughts didn't connect anymore. They were there and then gone. It was the strangest, most bizarre experience I've had. My brain has always been busy. Carrying out a task, while thinking and planning, remembering something else and listening to my internal music. Now, if I tried to remember something, there was a void. Nothing was recalled. I couldn't think properly either. I noticed one morning my facial skin didn't feel right; it didn't feel like mine. I had a minimal skincare routine and used a moisturiser, which had run out days before. Although my skin felt different, I didn't have the capacity to determine I needed to buy another bottle. Everything was a challenge. This was really brought home the day we dug up potatoes.

It was October; it had been raining, but the sun was in the sky. As the earth was wet, Dad decided it was time to dig up the potatoes (or tatties as we call them in Scotland) in my sister's large garden. She now lived in my paternal grandparents' house. I helped, while Mum supervised. Dad explained the strategy: he would take the fork and work down the hill, digging up the tattie shaws (the leaves above the ground) while I worked below him, collecting the tatties and putting them in a wire basket. So far, so good. I was ready. Dad dug, pushed and lifted, and potatoes spilled out, tumbling down the hill. I darted in one direction then, as the intended potato rolled past me, shot off in another direction. I pursued other potatoes heading in different directions. You've never seen such a random display of collection. Dad waited as I scrabbled around, gathering the remaining potatoes and putting them in the basket. He dug again. The same thing—more earth and potatoes poured down. Mum called out encouragement as I tried to catch plummeting potatoes, but again they evaded me. It was slow going, and I couldn't co-ordinate my movements. During a break I noticed Dad check the basket and remove seed potatoes, which I'd inadvertently included. As I looked at him blankly, he reminded me we didn't eat these. I knew what seed potatoes looked like, but I couldn't distinguish them when I gathered my bounty.

Back home, Mum suggested we clean the potatoes before storing them. I decided I could do this. Mum and Dad wanted me to go shopping with them instead, but this would be a big test. Not washing potatoes, but being on my own, the first time since I'd entered the river. I think they were anxious about leaving me. But I needed them to trust me, to know that I wasn't going to do anything similar. I'd be in the enclosed back garden. Nowhere for me to go. After discussion, Mum provided buckets, a dustsheet and a scrubbing brush, and they left.

Alone, I looked at the pile of potatoes and cleaning accoutrements. I tried to work out what to do. Normally only a quick glance would be needed. Now it seemed to take a lot of effort. Slowly I recognised I could create a production line with potatoes on one side of the buckets of water and the dustsheet on the other. It's painful to remember how difficult I found this simple task. The co-ordination of a few things was almost beyond me. Unimaginable. I filled the buckets, rolled up my sleeves, dipped a potato in the water and started to clean it between my hands. The water turned a dirty shade of brown. I picked up the scrubbing brush; I couldn't leave any dirt on the potato. Otherwise, what was the point of cleaning it? I rinsed each potato and soon had a small pile drying on the dust sheet. And too-full buckets filled with filthy water. I walked down the garden, slopping water and emptied them near Mum's camelia. Looking at the small pile of clean potatoes compared to the large dirty pile, I felt discouraged. How would I get through them all? Could I brush them just a little? I needed them to be clean; I couldn't leave them a little dirty. I had to be thorough. My hands turned red and my nose started to run. The autumn air turned colder.

The pile on the dustsheet grew, and I was pleased with my progress. My Heidi hat, a pink double-layered hat with ear coverings and long braids, slipped to the left of my head. I tried to rearrange it with the inside of my elbow. As I did, I saw Mum and Dad looking out the window. They'd been watching without me realising. The Scots have a word, *glaikit*, which means foolish or empty-headed. That's how I felt looking at them through the glass. They took a photo, me grinning, hat slightly askew, cheeks red with exertion, holding some prized clean potatoes. Mum came out and acclaimed my work. She was surprised because she'd intended only for the worst dirt to be taken off. Although Mum wanted to clean the remaining few, I was determined to complete the task. As I looked at my red, raw hands, I realised how cold I was. It was time to go inside.

My husband arrived early on the Saturday of the second weekend. He had sent me cards daily, saying he loved me and wished me a speedy recovery. I couldn't reply though. I couldn't put words together—at least not enough to write a letter. My vocabulary was basic, and I had difficulty constructing sentences. I've never been able to draw so I couldn't sketch 'letters' to him. Instead, I devised stick men and crude illustrations to depict what I did each week. The first 'letter' included the words 'shortbread!', 'knitting!', relaxation!', 'dominoes—Dad won!', 'walking!', 'making oatcakes and sausage rolls', 'some of the things I've been doing'. Associated pictures of candy floss trees, knitting needles, a ball of wool and a prone figure with some *zzzs* by it (to indicate me relaxing) accompanied the text. This period when I was unable to write sentences was alien. It underlined my deficiencies.

I was nervous about seeing him, aware of what I'd done and embarrassed by my state. When he arrived, he greeted Mum and Dad and then held out his arms. I walked into his embrace. He'd brought a present—a striped zebra soft toy. I held it close, looking at its glassy eyes, made to look incredibly sad. Despite knowing this, I didn't feel sadness. I still didn't feel anything.

That afternoon Mum, Dad, my sister, my husband and I went for a drive, all five of us squeezed in the car. We drove through hilly countryside, passed a sheepdog trial and parked by a stream. While my parents and sister went for a walk, my husband and I went down to the water. The grass tufts were spongy underfoot. I was careful not to fall in. We stood in a hug, watching the water flow. Not talking, just holding each other. Noticing some flat stones, my husband started to skim them into the stream. He began enthusiastically while I scrabbled around. Which stones would work? How flat did they need to be? I examined the stones almost forensically before picking some. My husband continued, and I watched as the stones bounced, bounced, bounced, bounced before disappearing under the water. I skimmed a stone and it promptly sank. Clearly not flat or round enough. I fumbled for more, but despite this being a favourite childhood pastime, none of my stones skimmed. My next 'letter' included a couple of circles and a square (depicting my useless, non-skimming selection) with the words 'skimming stones (?) with my sweetheart'.

I struggled to make sense of everything. Even though my family was around me, I didn't feel the way I usually did with them. I felt lonely. I listened to what they said. Watched as they laughed together. Joined in when given careful instructions about what to do. But it wasn't me. It was someone I didn't know. It was lonesome because no one else knew what I was experiencing. One day, walking from Gran's, my hand tucked in Mum's arm, I asked if this was the same as last time. Mum didn't ask what I meant. She knew exactly. She reassured me, squeezed my hand tightly and told me this time was different. When I had been ill years before, I had been physically unable to do things, but my mind had not been affected. Mum told me I would get better. Just as I had then. She was sure.

My sister had had a bat in her house. She couldn't stand bats or toads but now seemed to have both. I pricked up my ears. After my success hunting mice, we were moving on to bats, and I wanted to help! Mum and I checked behind the curtains in each room, pulling them closed and shaking them before re-opening them. Nothing, which was good. I hadn't considered what would happen if we found bats. How would we deal with them?

That night, as we sat knitting (I'd been promoted to knitting 'fish-and-chip' jumpers, to replace newspapers that mothers used to keep their babies warm in some of Africa's poorest areas) Mum reassured my sister she only had to worry about toads at her back door.

The next letter to my husband told him of my activities: 'hand-washing Gran's jumpers', 'hot soup (lentil) made today', 'me and Dad on a three-mile walk', 'an eight-inch finished square. Time to start another one', 'scone dough—to be made later today' and 'checking my sister's curtains for bats—none found thankfully'. Again I'd made some child-like drawings of a washing line with clothes hanging from it, a pan with marks above it to indicate heat, two stick figures (one tall) next to a road sign, some knitting on needles, a round circle with some dots (scone dough, the dots representing sultanas) and two oblongs hanging from a bar (the bat-free curtains). I thought this would show my husband I was busy.

The Crisis Team continued to visit. Mum and Dad joked that the notes they produced after each visit would be unique. Who else would have reference to making oatcakes and shortbread or wearing novelty hedgehog slippers? In truth, I wasn't making things. I wasn't doing anything on my own. Early on, Mum would take me from room to room. Kitchen to living room. Kitchen to bathroom. Living room to bed. Now, Mum weighed out ingredients, passed them to me and instructed when to add them. I took solace in beating or whisking, remembering how to cream mixtures or choosing the correct spoon (silver!) to fold in flour. My days were filled with activity. Just not determined by me. Mum and Dad directed what I would do. Ridiculous, isn't it? I was forty-one years old but could have been a small child. I needed reassurance, cuddles from Mum, repeated confirmation that I was doing well. Getting better. It just didn't seem that way.

I was devoid of feelings. Empty of everything. Nothing seemed to touch me or penetrate the void in my head. Earlier that summer, thirty-three Chilean miners had been trapped. Along with the rest of the world, I learned they were safe, but their rescue might take months. When the rescue was brought forward, there was constant TV coverage. Mum, Dad and I watched as miners were brought to the surface. Such a feat of engineering. Such immense willpower. Such a story of survival. And I watched it wordlessly. Unmoved. I could have been watching them alight at Victoria Station in London, having boarded one station before, for all the impact it had. While I recognised that they were being released from their private hell, a part of me wanted to know when I would be released from mine.

Lots of things changed during this period. Maybe due to the doses of medication I was taking, I don't know. One definite change was my inability to stay awake on a car journey. Usually I was alert, talking with fellow passengers, watching the countryside go past. Now, before we had left the village, I was nodding off. We were going to find a shed to accommodate the paraphernalia for Mum's new hobby: beekeeping. Sitting in the backseat with my sister, who was on holiday, I swayed as we went around corners, oblivious to the route or the beautiful scenery I was missing. I woke to the sound of dog barking, piercing my sleep. I noticed we were parked in a wood clearing and Mum and Dad weren't there before I resumed my slumber. I snoozed my way through negotiations on the best type of door frame, missed the placing of the order and was oblivious to advice on ground preparation for the shed erection. As we started the journey home, I barely noticed we were moving. The dog barking retreated in the distance as the car wheels turned.

Mum started keeping bees only three months before my breakdown, but she and Dad had attended meetings of the local Bee Club, she had an assigned 'bee buddy' (an experienced beekeeper to help and advise) and two hives of bees (collected in a dangerous mission after they swarmed) in my sister's garden. It was here, in the autumn sun with wonderful views over hills and woods, that I felt less on edge. I enjoyed the fresh, clean air—the perfect combination of slightly sharp but with velvety undertones—and the company of Mum, Dad, the bees and my sister, who provided a commentary on pollen collection, after carefully checking the colour chart.

I didn't know anything about beekeeping, but I joined Mum on a trip to a supplier. I dozed all the way there, arriving at the supplier without noticing any of the journey. I walked the aisles of unfamiliar products, feeling out of place and uncertain, feeling that I didn't belong. Did I question why things were unfamiliar? Did I ask myself, 'Why would I feel at home in a specialist equipment supplier?' No. I continued to feel disorientated as Mum paid and we left. These feelings were compounded when Mum and Dad declared us lost without a map! I tried to remain alert until we reached a helpful sign before resuming my slumberous state.

That night in bed I felt a weird sensation—my heart was beating very quickly. The usual, steady rhythm replaced by punchy, strong beats, the noise of which reverberated loudly through my head. What was happening? I began to worry something was wrong and tried to work out what to do. Get up? Get Mum? Was this a symptom of my illness? Would this happen regularly? Did I have pain? My heart pounded, fast and loud, and I lay unsure what to do. I tried to breathe deeply. Maybe that would help? My breath came out in pants. My heart bounced in my chest like it was on a pogo stick, and I breathed like I'd just run a mile. Remembering the relaxation CD, I tried to breathe like the woman encouraged me to do, but the erratic nature of my heartbeat was frightening. Something was wrong. Was it a panic attack? I'd never had one before. I remembered I had diazepam on my bedside table. Although I didn't want to become reliant on tablets, I took one with water and lay back down. Almost immediately I felt calmer, my heartbeat not so loud in my head. Although it continued to beat strongly, its frantic, frenetic pace was slowing. Tablets couldn't work that quickly, could they? Maybe it was the effect of taking a tablet? I knew there was a word to describe that but couldn't think what it was. I lay, covers loosely around me, cast off when I'd felt hot. I was aware my heartbeat was becoming less noticeable. Less loud. Less prominent in the quiet night. I felt disappointed I'd taken a tablet to feel better. Why couldn't I help myself without medication? Was it normal to take tablets in such circumstances? Did other people? Without answers but with a slowing heartbeat, I tried to fall asleep again.

Not many people knew I was with Mum and Dad. I was there, but almost not. The first few weeks were all about medication, keeping busy, doing little tasks, calling my husband, going to my sister's garden and walking to visit Gran. On my way there one day, I met one of Dad's Paths Group buddies. Since retiring, Dad has been a member of a dedicated volunteer group, working with local landowners to build and maintain paths in the beautiful countryside around the village. Dad's friend stopped to chat, and I haltingly told him I wasn't well, that I might be depressed. He was sorry to hear that. We talked briefly before going our separate ways. Later, he told Dad it was good that I could still talk to people.

Occasionally Mum would take me shopping, but I found this overwhelming. There was too much choice in the supermarket. How did Mum know what to choose? What was good value? Why did she buy some items in smaller shops? This was when I noticed I was living a life that I didn't understand any more. Everyone else seemed to go about their business happily enough. I couldn't.

One night in bed, after playing the relaxation CD and taking my medication, I became aware of a strange sensation in the left side of my head, as it rested on the pillow. Suddenly, a loud 'ping' followed by a lesser, duller 'ping' went off in my head, like a rubber band snapping. It was weird, like something in my head had detached itself. Lying in the dark, I tried to reassure myself this was good. Maybe I was getting better? On the road to recovery? Soon back to the Ali of old? I turned over and hoped sleep would come.

Although I didn't go out much, people visited Mum and Dad and I tried to talk to them. Mum's bee buddy liked to pop in to discuss the progress of her hives. Tea, scones and cakes would be handed round. Mum has always been a prodigious baker. When Dad went on a charity trek to Nepal with his cousin, Mum and his wife raised the necessary funds (and more!) by baking. Mum had shown me how to make pastry for an apple pie, and I lined an old tin plate (the pink nail varnish a give-away to its history). I peeled and cored the apples Mum gave me and filled the pie, before sugaring the fruit and adding the top. Although Mum supervised its making and baking, she told her bee buddy it was my pie.

I realised I didn't have Mum's recipes, so she gave me a small black book to copy down recipes I particularly liked. Dad introduced me to the world of soup-making, his domain, and I added instructions on using the pressure cooker. Savoury recipes were written at the front of the book and cakes and sweets at the back. Dad always made our Christmas cake and used the same early 1970s women's magazine recipe each year. He seemed to love weighing the fruit, checking and cleaning it, and preparing the mixture. Once baked, he wrapped the cake and fed it (with brandy!) at regular intervals. He produced the most delicious, moist cakes. A couple of years before, Christmas celebrations were threatened—his recipe was lost, possibly recycled by mistake. We tried to remember the ingredients and measurements but couldn't. Before writing to the magazine for help, salvation came in the shape of Gran. On hearing of its loss, she directed my sister upstairs in her cottage to a pile of magazines, including the exact issue in which the recipe was contained. See, she said, it paid not to throw things away!

As I had completed numerous fish-and-chip baby jumpers, Mum decided I needed a new knitting project. She disappeared and returned with needles, wool and a pattern. I was going to knit a cape, she declared! Mum was a fan of capes. They were a staple of her wardrobe; different colours and textures, ready to be thrown over whatever she was wearing. I'm not such a fan. Sure, I had a poncho in the 1970s (who didn't?) but no capes. All the better, Mum said. I'd have a new addition to my wardrobe when complete!

I listened as Mum instructed me on the number of cast-on stitches, concentrating hard. Compared to the squares and fish-and-chip baby jumpers, the cape had so many more stitches. The cream-coloured wool felt soft as it moved through my hands, but the little knobbles running through it meant I had to concentrate even harder as I pulled the wool through to make stitches. The pattern worked from the bottom upwards, so I cast on stitch after stitch until my needle was filled. Counting them proved difficult and I interrupted Mum's wall-hanging work (progressing nicely) to double-check I had the requisite number. She took over the needles and counted. We didn't agree! I tried to cram on a few more stitches before we checked again. Satisfied I had the correct number, I began to knit my first-ever cape.

The shed for the bee paraphernalia was due to arrive. So, we needed to level the ground in my sister's garden to accommodate it. Dressed for action and with my Heidi hat on, despite the winter sun, I was ready to help. I awaited instructions while standing, armed with a spade and in charge of the wheelbarrow. Mum and Dad confidently marked out the ground and started to take off the top layer of grass. Working as a team, Dad broke a sod of grass and Mum or I put it in the wheelbarrow; we developed a rhythm. When the wheelbarrow was full, I pushed it to the compost heap, carefully tipping it out (mindful of the hedgehog, preparing to hibernate there).

Things were going well. Then Mum and Dad decided they needed to dig deeper into the slope. I looked around as they discussed this, as I couldn't add anything to the conversation. I'd hated maths at school and, even if I'd been well, couldn't have commented on angles and depth. Salvation arrived just in time (Mum and Dad were increasingly exasperated) in the form of my younger uncle and cousin. Mum had asked them to help, anticipating they'd be needed!

My cousin quickly took charge, checking the proposed location and measurements of the shed and marking it out with long poles he'd brought. We'd been in the garden for some time and didn't seem to have accomplished much, but my cousin provided fresh impetus. I repositioned the wheelbarrow as Mum, Dad and I resumed our roles. Lifting a particularly large shovel full of soil, I swung round, intending to fill the wheelbarrow. I missed. It tipped over and my cousin and uncle laughed. Any other time I would have joined in. I watched as the soil rolled down the hill, but I couldn't laugh. I felt so helpless, as if I couldn't do anything. I felt my heart begin to race as I stumbled around, trying to right and refill the wheelbarrow. A tree branch brushed my head. I continued forward. My Heidi hat didn't. It was left behind, hooked on the branch, dangling there. Cue even more laughter from my cousin and uncle. And this time Mum and Dad joined in.

I was standing in crisp, fresh air under the autumnal sun. The joyful sounds of laughter from people I loved surrounded me. All I wanted to do was cry. But no tears came. Instead, I blundered about, trying to retrieve my hat and reposition the wheelbarrow. I was shaking so much, my movements uncoordinated. Mum quietly told me to stop and go with her to the car. To continued laughter, I allowed Mum to lead me up the garden steps. She explained to the others that we were going to have a tea break. Quietly she told me I was going to take some medication. I looked at her blankly—I had taken my tablets that morning, what was she talking about? 'You need some diazepam', she said. I disagreed. 'Yes, you do, Ali', she said. 'You know we were told only to take some when necessary, well this is one of those times.' Was it? Why couldn't I tell? I didn't want to take more and more tablets and so I continued to disagree. However, Mum was having none of it. I needed some diazepam. Finally, we compromised. I took half a tablet. As I did so, I wondered what had become of me. Someone who had to be led out a garden for medication. Who couldn't see what was funny, when others laughed. We sat in the car for some time, not really talking, just sitting there. Back down in the garden, we found my cousin had finished the job. As he left, I thanked him for all his help. We'd been struggling before he arrived. He looked at me gently and reminded me that work like this was much more his skill set than mine.

My uncle had said my big cousin was visiting and wanted to see me. I felt some trepidation. I hadn't seen her for some time, and she would expect the old me. Someone I wasn't now. Someone I didn't know if I would be ever again. In the car with Mum and Dad, we saw my aunt and two cousins going for a walk. They waved and I waved back. We were only a few feet away, but it felt like miles. Waving to each other through extra thick glass. Everything a little distorted. Unclear. Not in the moment. It wasn't just glass that separated us. It was so much more. Me and my illness. I realised my uncle and cousin had probably relayed what had happened in the garden, explained that I had to be led away for medication and confirmed that I wasn't myself. The distance between us, as our car drove away, wasn't just physical.

Although I had hoped the two 'pings' in my head, which I had felt in bed, would herald an improvement, it seemed to be the opposite. I began to worry about the future of my marriage, that I wouldn't be able to look after myself in the future and about all the things I couldn't do. Mum tried to reassure me. I would get better. Everything would be OK. I was still a capable person. Really? I heard what she said, but I couldn't believe her. I became fixated on two things I didn't think I could do. As we both worked full-time, my husband and I had self-designated chores, some we did separately, others together. We shopped and cooked together, catching up on the day and, while I poured drinks, my husband served the meal. Somehow my brain ignored these everyday his-and-hers tasks and turned them into a 'he can, I can't' situation.

Mum seemed bemused when I said I needed to learn how to spoon potatoes onto a plate. She stood back as I tried to wrangle the mince out of the pan to join the potatoes. She stepped in once I was finished and said she would dish up the rest! Each night I was determined to put whatever she had cooked onto my plate myself—almost as if this demonstrated I was getting better.

My sister took me to buy petrol so I could learn how to fill up the car. My chivalrous husband usually bought petrol for me but, again, my mind told me I couldn't do it myself. Nothing and no one would make me believe differently. My younger sister instructed me: 'Open the petrol cap, choose the right fuel, insert the nozzle correctly, fill it up.' Leaning on her car, watching the dial change, waiting for the expected click, I decided I would need to do this with her a few more times. Then I might be able to do it myself.

Despite this, I was convinced I wasn't getting better. I'd never get better. I'd never enjoy the things I had before. I couldn't remain married when I couldn't do anything for myself. I needed to be looked after, but I couldn't expect my husband to look after me. There seemed to be no way out. I was facing a frightening and uncertain future. I was at the end of my tether and didn't want to continue living like this.

Mum noticed I was becoming increasingly negative. We sat in the kitchen after breakfast and I told Mum and Dad about all the things I used to be able to do, things that I couldn't do now. I couldn't go on. Mum became upset and got up to make soup; Dad went to read the newspaper in the living room. It was just Mum and me.

I sat on the bench behind the table, watching her. In front of the sink, framed by the window and the blue sky outside, birds were flying into the garden and perching on the washing line. Lining up for their turn at the feeders, wobbling in the wind. Mum spoke as she began to peel carrots, telling me that she knew I would get better. She sobbed as she told me she couldn't imagine her life and the world without me in it. I sat motionless. With great heaving sobs and chunks of carrot flying in different directions (peeling had turned into uncontrolled hacking), she said she couldn't imagine how awful I must feel to want to end my life. And she knew she couldn't stop me. If I really wanted to do it, then there was nothing she could do. Gulping and crying, with birds still visiting the garden, she said she couldn't imagine not wanting to wake up, not to want to see the sky and the sun, the birds and the trees—all the lovely things of nature. If I truly wanted to leave the world, then I had to do it, but she needed me to know the effect it would have on her.

I still sat. Ordinarily when someone was upset, I'd want to offer comfort. Now, I was struck by my numbness. I should want to put my arms around Mum and tell her everything was going to be OK. I watched as her sobs and hiccups eased slightly and the offending carrot was placed on the board to be cut. I had to go to her. I got up, moved across the kitchen and put my arm around her in a half hug as we both stood, looking at the birds, flying in and out freely. I needed to reassure her. Needed her not to worry about me, despite how I was feeling. I promised I wouldn't try to harm myself again without seeking help.

I didn't want to continue living the way I was, but that didn't mean I wanted to leave the world. I just wanted to be me again.

The dog next door kept barking. Added to our morning ritual of newspapers, commentary and tablets, Mum remarked how many times she'd heard the dog bark during the night. It happened during the day, too. Returning after coffee with Gran, there would be howling. As we prepared lunch, there would be barking. Later, Dad reading his paper (still), Mum continuing her wall-hanging (the beach finished, the tree taking shape), me concentrating on knitting my cape (slowly), there would be accompanying yowling.

One evening Mum had enough. She couldn't cope any longer. She was going around to our neighbour. Dad and I sat in silence as we heard the faint ring of a doorbell, then nothing. A few seconds later Mum returned and continued to watch television. After more loud barking, she announced she was going to see if our neighbour was visiting his daughter. Dad and I looked at each other, neither of us wanting her to go alone, so I followed Mum.

We stood on a nearby doorstep, the sound of barking still in our ears. There was no response, so Mum set off in another direction—perhaps our neighbour was visiting friends? Another doorstep, Mum in front, me standing behind. When the door opened, I popped up like a meerkat above Mum's left shoulder as she explained why we were there. Although they couldn't help, they said they would call someone who looked after the dog if our neighbour was away. I clutched Mum's arm, knowing that normally something like this wouldn't bother her at all. But now it seemed the barking was like a dripping tap, once heard, the noise magnified. Becoming more annoying as attention focused on it, the noise anticipated. I realised my situation was wearing Mum down and affecting her behaviour and that of my family. We said goodnight and I walked home with Mum, holding her arm, trying to give some support.

My husband had asked me to arrange a delivery of flowers on his behalf, so I was going to the new village flower shop. Usually I was with Mum, Dad or my sister, so I felt a bit daunted as I entered the florist on my own. Inside there was a wonderful display of flowers, associated greenery and floral art arrangements, quite different to the newspaper order book, magazine racks and large bottles of sweets I remembered from the former newsagents there. As if speaking underwater, my voice fuzzy in my head, I spoke to the florist, who suggested I look through a large book containing bouquets of all shapes, sizes and costs. I flicked the pages, choosing one arrangement before turning another page. Oh no, wait. I preferred the next bouquet. I continued to look through the book and changed my mind again, before giving my order. The florist looked at my choice before suggesting another one. I agreed to the change. Why couldn't I be decisive? I was usually clear about what I liked or disliked and didn't need guidance on something like this. As the florist began to complete the order form, she broke off to show me one further recommendation. Again, I changed my mind. No hesitation. Why was I changing my mind repeatedly? Why couldn't I decide on my own and stick with my decision? I quickly gave the woman the delivery details, dictated a short message and paid before I could be persuaded to change my mind again. On the walk home, I puzzled over my indecision and the way I had been so easily influenced.

Mum co-ordinated the annual poppy collection and she dispatched Dad to bring down the collecting paraphernalia from the attic, ready for the upcoming collection. The village and outlying areas had specific routes, and Mum had a team of willing collectors to help. First, she needed to make sure everything was in order—numbering tins, putting stickers on them, and documenting the tin assignment to route and collector.

We sat on the living room floor together, with tins, stickers, poppies and lists surrounding us. I stickered tins while Mum busied herself allocating new collectors to routes and preparing lists. I listened as she told me who was doing each route. I was familiar with the people and street names and had collected around the village before, so I could envisage what she described. Mum began to frown as I read out the tin numbers for her to record. Something was amiss. She called a halt, while she reviewed our work, and I scrabbled across the floor for a recalcitrant tin that had rolled away from my sticking area and was heading towards the sofa.

Things didn't seem to match up. Why not? As Mum went to make herself a coffee (her solution for everything) I took the lists and tried to check what she had written. Reviewing documents, checking for accuracy, identifying inconsistencies and duplication was like bread and butter to me. All my work roles had required attention to detail. Still, nothing seemed to make sense. I was frustrated; this should be a simple, quick task. Retrieving another tin from under a chair, I stood them all in one place, to avoid the making-a-bid-for-freedom exercise that they seemed to have colluded in. Why hadn't I done that before? Why couldn't I co-ordinate stickers and tins without them going walkabout? I shared my frustration with Mum, who suggested I drink a cup of tea while she worked things out. I took up my knitting and watched as Mum reassembled everything and set to work. I had only done a few rows when she pronounced herself finished. Really? That quickly? I began to realise I had possibly been a hindrance, but Mum brushed this aside and insisted I could help with deliveries. That afternoon found us in the car, tootling around the village and local country estates, with me ready to hand over tins and instructions when we came to a stop. Despite my 'help', it seemed that a collection would take place!

I had worked steadily on my cape, knitting slowly, repeatedly calling Mum over to catch dropped stitches, count rows and deal with the vagaries of sewing up. I loved knitting, but I wasn't keen on sewing up and often Mum or Gran helped. Mum insisted she would instruct this time, but I should sew the buttonhole bands to the cape. I struggled and toiled; I wasn't a natural sewer and it took a long time. Thank goodness there weren't more pieces. Finally, I sewed on the last button and ta-da—I had a cape! Mum immediately asked me to try it on and so, to much appreciation, I modelled it to Mum and Dad. It felt warm, hung loosely around me, swirled when I turned. I liked it. One side of the buttonhole band was longer than the other. When I pointed out this deficiency to Mum, she said no one would notice. If they did, it showed it was an individual piece. I'd done it! With guidance and help. Nevertheless, I'd finished the cape.

My sister's garden must be one of the most peaceful places there is—sloped behind her house, the rooftops of houses opposite with hills, fields and woods beyond beautifully visible. As I sat at the top of her garden, watching buzzards soar over trees, then hover as they eyed some prey, I thought how free they looked. They glided peacefully, glorious to watch, but contrasting with the restless energy I felt locked up inside me. How could I sit somewhere so tranquil, yet feel so agitated? As I watched smaller birds fly to the feeders in the garden, the buzzards floating in the distance, I was desperate to be free too. I didn't know how to achieve freedom, but it was in that idyllic garden I made a phone call to a counsellor recommended by my employer. I had to go home. I had to get well. I had to find peace. Even though I was scared about how I would be without my parents and sister, how I would pass the time when my husband was at work, how I would cope without being told when and how to do things, I had to go home.

My husband had arranged my flight and so we were standing in the airport, with me wearing my 'depression cape' as I'd started to call it. I didn't have luggage to check in; I'd brought only a few things six weeks before. I knew I had to go home, but I was scared. What would I do? How would I know what to do? My head still didn't feel like it belonged to me. I'd been surrounded by family, been cared for and looked after, been told what to do, when and how. Now I was boarding a plane on my own. Mum reassured me that my husband would meet me, so I wouldn't be on my own for long.

We stood at the bottom of stairs leading to departures, a little huddle amongst the determined travellers heading for their flights or cars. Mum continued to cuddle me, while Dad looked on, as I said that I didn't want to go. Through tears, Mum said she didn't want me to go either, but I would get the treatment I needed back home. I thanked them for looking after me during such a horrible time and Mum said that we'd got through it, largely because I'd done what I was told. I hadn't questioned or argued, I'd just blithely acquiesced. We hugged one last time and I started to climb the stairs, turning to wave until I couldn't see them any longer.

CHAPTER 4

November 2010 – Struggling

From that point I had to concentrate. I was on my own—no one to rely on to tell me where to go or what to do. I felt baffled and confused by security, even though I'd flown before. Where to put my ticket? Should I take off my cape? Would my small rucksack go in a tray or on the conveyor belt? I was hesitant and unsure, not wanting to do the wrong thing. Thankfully, it wasn't busy and, having navigated my way through security, I made my way towards the duty-free area. I didn't know what to do. Should I sit? Where? How would I know when to board? I felt completely alone and uneasy. I couldn't sit and relax, so instead I propped myself up against the wall and watched the screen. Every few minutes I checked that I still had my ticket.

Boarding the plane, I tried to find my row, aware that I would need to put my rucksack and cape in the overhead locker, but not wanting to inconvenience other passengers. Ducking into the row, I removed my cape and tried to put the rucksack up. My first attempt failed. There wasn't enough room for me to swing it up and gain momentum. I tried to work out when the next gap in passengers would be and took advantage of some early row ticket holders. In two uncoordinated moves, I placed my rucksack in the locker and threw my cape on top. The cape began to slide and dangle down towards me. Feebly, I tried to stuff it back in, up on my tiptoes to gain maximum purchase. It looked like it might stay, so I quickly sat back down, ready to buckle up.

After landing I walked with other travellers, although I felt very distinct from them, to the arrivals hall. I wasn't sure where to go or how to exit but was reassured that I was following others. As we reached a small conveyor belt, the people in front came to a halt. I tried to pass them, without being noticeable or needing them to move. As I walked through the crowd, I realised no one else was walking. Everyone had stopped to collect luggage. I began to wonder where I would exit. How would I get there? Would I go the wrong way? What if I went the wrong way? Where would I end up? I was becoming more and more fretful when I noticed that the corridor split into two. Which way should I go? Why were there no signs? If I slowed down, would other passengers overtake me? I turned but there was no one in sight.

The fork was coming up. Which way? Right or left? I tried to keep my feet moving, but they were reluctant. Which way? Which way? Right or left? I couldn't decide, but suddenly saw a man appear from the left, walking towards me. He was followed by another man and then a whole group of people. My feet started to move again as I snuck in behind, keen to blend in with this purposeful group, who knew where they were going.

Double doors burst open as the first man approached, leading us into an open, poorly lit area. I continued to walk, scanning the waiting throng for my husband. I stole furtive glances around the families and individuals before noticing someone move forward from their leaned stance against a pillar. Relief. It was my husband. He surrounded me in a big hug, making me feel safe and significant, not letting me go. He whispered how glad he was that I was back and how much he had missed me, before taking my rucksack. With his arm around me, we walked out, my husband shielding me from overzealous luggage-trolley-pushers. I began to feel a little more comfortable amongst the people and noise. Keeping me tight against him, my husband said he had feared I wouldn't come back. I couldn't find the words to tell him that even though I was there, it wasn't really me who was back.

Before leaving my parents', I had arranged a doctor's appointment, which my husband would take me to before going to work. I wanted to get better. Maybe this appointment would help me on my way? Shortly before we left, my neighbour called round to give me a bouquet of flowers. As I thanked her, my husband put the flowers in a vase. I continued to get ready while I heard her say that she and her husband were there to help, any time. As she left, she gripped my hand, saying, 'We'll get through this'. Why did she seem so confident? Did she not know what I was going through?

We sat in the waiting room, my husband reading something for work, me just looking around. I was pleased I would be seeing my regular doctor, even though I normally attended her other surgery. After calling me to the consulting room, she confirmed that the doctors in Scotland had sent down some notes. She asked how I was doing, if I was sleeping, what medication I was on? She listened and, on hearing that I was having difficulty sleeping, prescribed me sleeping tablets. We discussed the anti-depressants I had been prescribed and she suggested a different tablet. I just wanted to be better. If she thought this medication would help, then I would take it. As she gave me another sickness certificate for work, she asked if I had a project to keep me busy. I said no. I wasn't sure what I could do. She suggested I take up a new sport, perhaps badminton? She, like everyone else, reassured me I would get better.

My husband dropped me off at the chemist on his way to work. The grey-suited pharmacist called my name and came around the counter to stand beside me, before gently asking if I had taken these tablets before. When I responded in the negative, he slowly explained the dosage and frequency to me. He was so kind and careful to make sure I understood, before taking my payment.

Despite the route home being familiar, everything else was alien. As I was usually at work during the week, I wasn't used to the everyday hustle and bustle. People were all around. Cars in the streets, pedestrians on the pavements, commuters descending the stairs to the station. I didn't know about weekday activity outside work. I didn't know our hometown buzzed and hummed while I sat in an office. Just another thing I didn't know. That night I took my first sleeping tablet. The taste was horrible even though I tried to swallow it quickly. I succumbed to a deep sleep only to wake up next morning with the same horrible taste in my mouth.

I resumed some of the usual housework—washing (clothes hung up inside due to the rain) and cooking. I wanted to have soup, homemade like Mum and Dad's rather than out a tin. I'd tried to make soup before, but generally I was left with a mass of vegetables and no liquid. So, for the first time, I decided to use the pressure cooker that Mum had previously given me. Truth be told, I'd been scared to use it without supervision. I remembered from childhood the panic when steady hissing turned into a raging growl, usually accompanied by Mum and Gran advancing like an army towards the enemy, armed with tea towels to contain the impending attack. Their moves were well-rehearsed and well-orchestrated, and once they'd subdued the pressure cooker, smothering it under towels and moving it to a non-heated ring, we could all begin to breathe again. These memories were present as I took my first tentative steps towards pressure cooker use. I followed the recipe for Dad's leek and potato soup—remembering to sweat the vegetables first. Despite having watched Mum and Gran, I struggled to put on the pressure cooker lid. Finally, I engaged the lid just at the right part of the pan, turned it, and it was on.

I waited to see when I needed to add weights, watching as black liquid began to spurt out the top. Shooting off in all directions. The splashback. The lights above. As the pressure rose, the sputtering gained momentum. I began to breathe rapidly, fearing a black eruption that would mess up the kitchen, possibly damage the cooker-hood and—who knew?—maybe the ceiling above. Mum would know what to do. I ran to my phone and Dad answered my call. He told Mum that I needed her, that the pressure cooker was firing black liquid jets all over the kitchen. Mum was at a critical stage of making tablet (a Scottish sugar-laden delicacy) and had to beat it continuously until smooth. She couldn't come to the phone but, through Dad, told me to advance, switch off the gas and aim a towel at the top of the pan. I did as she instructed, gradually breathing easier as the weights steadied. Under the towel, there was only muffled hissing. I explained to Dad there'd be no soup that evening, and pressure cooking was going to have to wait.

That first week back with my husband was strange. I wasn't used to being the way I was—not able to think or do—and things didn't feel normal. My husband suggested I establish a routine to help the days pass. The Crisis Team had told me to have a regular time to get up, and I stuck to that religiously. Over breakfast I watched *Wanted Down Under*, a show about families considering emigration to Australia or New Zealand. Then I watched *Homes Under the Hammer*, seeing different properties up for auction and renovation across the country. After this, I walked into town to shop before lunch. The mornings took care of themselves, but I found the afternoons difficult to fill. I knew I needed to do something. Meet people. But I wasn't sure how. I had become used to being with my family, having people around me. Now there was just the two of us and during the day, I was on my own.

I saw posters advertising an information day for local charities and groups. Getting involved in the community seemed to be the answer. My husband agreed to come, and we visited the stands, me with an awkward grin on my face and fear in my heart that people would try to engage me in conversation. I wouldn't be able to answer coherently; my vocabulary was still limited. I signed up for a newsletter on local environmental projects and paid money to join some groups, but I couldn't see myself getting involved. I didn't feel 'fit' or suitable to be in company. Although I was in a busy hall, I felt as if I was hovering above everyone and looking at the scene through a stranger's eye. Although I had hoped to feel enthusiastic and interested in what we had seen and done, nothing registered as we left. No emotion, no enthusiasm, nothing.

Next day, feeling unusually disconnected from my husband, I suggested we go for a walk on the local common. We donned walking boots and parked in an unfamiliar area to explore somewhere new. We walked through the trees and mud, branches crunching under foot, with little conversation. We always talked, so this semi-silent stroll was strange. It enhanced my feelings of unease. Detachment. Unhappiness. After a while, my husband suggested we turn and so we trudged back in the autumn afternoon. Nearing the car, I felt I needed to say something. To acknowledge my husband taking me out. I said it had been a lovely walk, but he looked at me and said he wasn't sure he agreed.

Since university, I had always worked full-time. I had moved from job to job and was used to earning my way, even though our finances were joint. This period of not working and receiving statutory benefits was alien to me. Another pressure. I asked my husband if we could still meet our financial obligations. We sat together while he checked our bank statements, identified our outgoings and assessed whether our lowered income could sustain us. I began to talk about how I was feeling, how worried I was that I wasn't working, disturbing him as he tried to concentrate. Finally, his exasperation grew, and he told me to stop. I had asked him to check whether we would be OK financially. He was trying to do this. My constant talking wasn't helping, and he needed me to be quiet. As he continued to study the figures, I lost interest, got up and went into another room. After a while he came to reassure me that we would manage. Things would be tight, but we hadn't overextended ourselves. We had some savings. I should focus on getting better and not worry about money.

Often on Sundays I'd prepare a meal while my husband worked in the garden. As there were few ingredients and I'd watched Mum make one, I decided on fish pie. I checked I had all the ingredients before following Mum's instructions to make a roux. Despite memories of my last unsuccessful attempt at making a sauce, everything looked promising. As I poured the thick mixture into my green casserole dish, I watched it land in the centre of the dish and . . . stay there. No movement. Nothing to the left. Nothing to the right. No spread across the casserole base. That would have to do; I needed the rest of the sauce to cover the fish. I swirled two pieces of river cobbler through the mixture in the dish before spooning on the 'remainder'. Rather than being smothered under a blanket of sauce, small blobs sat proudly on top of the fish. Still, very obviously fish-like. What to do? I quickly hacked the skinned tomato, while I held it with a fork. Did it matter that some bits were chunky? Others see-through? The kitchen took on the appearance of *The Muppet Show* as I wielded knives like the Swedish chef. Next, the cheese. Soon slices, thin at the top and thick at the bottom (I could never cut cheese straight), were arranged over the tomato. Finally, I needed to add mashed potatoes. No amount of pressure mashed them, so instead I sliced the potatoes. After a few minutes of slashing through the pan, I poured the potatoes on top of the cheese, followed by about half a pint of milk to make it look smoother (and less dry!). Feeling in control, I put the pie in the oven and set the timer.

I started to tidy up the mess—pans, knives, chopping board, measuring jugs and forks. The kitchen looked like a battlefield. When my husband came in, he asked what we were eating. Fish pie and broccoli, I replied. He looked at the cooker, its top empty apart from four gas rings. I followed his gaze. I hadn't prepared the broccoli. How had I forgotten? I knew I wanted to serve it. Why wasn't it cooking? I set to it, but we had fish stuck to the bottom of the casserole, wedges of tomato in a cheesy-milky soup with lumpy potato and hard broccoli for lunch.

Domestic bliss wasn't restricted to fish pie. My husband suggested a challenge—how much money could I save on our shopping bill? We agreed I would drive to our usual supermarket, check prices and then go to the budget store in town. I felt tense and detached as I drove. I jotted down prices, before leaving empty-handed to do a price comparison at the other store. It was disconcerting, not knowing where things where. The different packaging befuddled me. My intended price-comparison task seemed impossible because of different brands and sizes. This was so unfamiliar—like crossing your arms the wrong way. Have you ever tried that? We all fold our arms one way, one over the other, some right over left, others left over right. Now swap them. That's how I felt—completely wrong.

Instead of comparing, I had two separate lists. That night my husband suggested a different strategy—try to find offers. Next day as I walked past the butcher's shop, I noticed the price of half a dozen eggs. It looked like a good deal, so I went in. Looking around, I spied a tray of liver. That was cheap, wasn't it? I bought enough for two and walked on to the discount store. This time the floor-to-ceiling cardboard boxes weren't so daunting. I bought potatoes and cabbage and, noticing everyone put their items back in the basket or trolley before packing their bags at a bench, I did the same.

Although my experiences in the kitchen hadn't been successful (to put it mildly) and producing edible meals, fruit crumbles and chocolate cakes was a dim, distant memory, I tried to persevere. I knew liver needed to be coated in seasoned flour before frying. I started to boil the potatoes and cabbage before getting the liver underway. The kitchen smelled of that distinctive aroma of boiled cabbage. The liver sizzled and spat at me and soon frying offal overpowered the smell of boiling cabbage. The smell was pervasive. The air became thick. Only the shrieking of the fire alarm could pierce through it. My husband ran in, cursed quietly and opened doors, before wafting a tea towel vigorously beneath the alarm. I stood by the spitting pan, helpless. Gradually, the fog cleared. The alarm relented to a few gently pinging reminders of my latest culinary attempt. I drained the potatoes and cabbage, dished it up and we ate my latest offering.

Undeterred and realising that we had cabbage left, I returned to the butchers. I bought more liver. Why not something else? Don't ask me. It was like being conditioned to buy the cheapest cut of meat. Maybe the butcher would have suggested something as cheap. I didn't think to ask.

The second night of liver cooking was less adventurous. My husband was surprised when he saw our meal. Déjà vu! I felt quite pleased with myself. A meal without the cacophony of smoke alarms.

My husband asked if we could eat something other than liver. He hadn't eaten it in years. Twice in two nights was probably enough. Good point. When I was at work, we usually ate quick, varied meals. So, again, I went to the butchers and this time I bought sausages. Fearing a repeat of the fire alarm drama, I cooked them in the oven. Soon sausages, potatoes and cabbage were served up. Well, there was still cabbage left, so why not? After three nights of cabbage, my husband suggested a new challenge: different meat and vegetables every evening!

As I struggled for things to do during the day, my husband suggested a jigsaw. Not the kind where you recreate a picture, but where you work out what it might look like in the future or from a different perspective. We have a bit of a jigsaw protocol—separate the edge pieces, build the jigsaw frame, declare there are missing edge pieces and double-check the remaining pieces to find the offenders. When the frame is complete, my husband uses faces, colours or patterns to build up areas, while I find individual pieces based on shape.

I tried to find pieces for the jigsaw we'd started. The task seemed strange. I was used to finding the one piece needed to finish an area. Nonetheless, I thought I should attempt my husband's jigsaw role. I decided to do it in a—, no, the word wouldn't come. I needed to work in a certain way. Although the word began with *s*, I couldn't remember it. I looked over pieces, trying to find colours, mulling over the word.

The jigsaw was forgotten, my focus on remembering the word. It was '*s*—'. I was going to do the jigsaw in a '*s*—' way. I knew that people forgot words and it wasn't a big deal, but I hadn't used a lot of different words recently. The inability to get the word was magnified. My head was empty, nothing there.

Just as I was about to give up, like a runner powering through the finish line, arms flailing from the momentum, the word 'structured' burst into my mind. That was it. I was going to do the jigsaw in a structured way. It was a long word and I felt pleased that I'd got it. Structured. That was it. Deciding the jigsaw no longer held my interest, I went out for a walk.

When I recounted the day to my husband, I told him about the search for, and the finding of, the missing word 'structured'. As I told him about the quest for the *s* word, suddenly 'structured' didn't seem right after all. Satisfaction dimmed. My husband looked over and asked whether I meant to do the jigsaw in a *systematic* way? Ah, right. Systematic. That was the word.

I drove to my first counselling session, in my counsellor's home a short way across town. As I entered, her cat tried to wind its way round my legs. Soon I was telling her more about what happened in Scotland and how I was feeling. Had I ever been scared or anxious about something, but had overcome my fear? I wasn't a fan of flying and I'd get very nervous, especially before take-off. My palms would suddenly leak water and I usually had to clutch tissues to avoid soaking the arm rests and seat. The strange noises of the plane on my first flight had worried me. Gradually, as I'd flown more and become accustomed to the thrust of engines on take-off and the sound of the landing gear moving into place before touch-down, I'd felt more relaxed. My palms less sweaty. The counsellor explained I had overcome my anxiety about flying and I would overcome it in this case too.

She asked me to remember how I felt when I was in my happy place— where I felt most relaxed. That's what I was to work towards: relaxation. But where was my happy place? When did I feel relaxed? The counsellor recommended a book about overcoming anxiety and asked me to keep a thought diary. We would discuss it at our next session. I should record my thoughts, describe the situation, the physical sensations I experienced (on an intensity rating of 0–100%), my mood (on an intensity rating of 0–100%), what was going through my mind just before, the believability of these automatic thoughts (on a believability rating of 0–100%) and any associated thoughts, memories, images or ideas.

I stared blankly at the piece of paper she gave me; it seemed so complicated. There were no examples, but the counsellor explained that, just like a diary, I didn't need to record every thought. Just the important ones. I stared at her. She didn't know me. Aside from my current situation, I had another problem. I didn't keep a diary. Not that I'd never tried; I still have my diary from 1984. Every entry started with 'got up'. Hmmm, slightly self-evident. I stopped by mid-March. I knew it was meant to be about interesting or exciting things, but I seemed to need to write everything. I couldn't work out what to record.

My childhood best friend kept a diary and I was always slightly envious that she'd be able to look back, remember and giggle about things she'd done. I had plainly missed out on the 'diary-keeping' gene, but I resolved to get the recommended book and keep a thought diary before our next appointment.

The Crisis Team had stressed the importance of relaxation too. Every day I would lie on the sofa, listening to the quietly spoken woman as she encouraged me to tense and relax. Was I beginning to relax? It didn't seem so. Mum and I had started yoga classes after I'd stopped running, and I remembered how we'd breathe deeply. Stretch into different contorted positions. Lie on our backs with blankets over us at the end of the session, while the instructor talked quietly about our muscles softening throughout our bodies. How sometimes there was gentle snoring from a classmate. I knew I could be relaxed. I just didn't know how to get there now.

After another unsuccessful session, when I seemed to be tenser than at the start, I was beginning to resent the narrator. I became aware of my chest tightening. What was happening? The tightness moved down my stomach, pelvis and into my legs to be replaced by a steady, continual buzzing. It's hard to describe, but it felt like electricity charging my body. Humming insistently. Pressure moving down my legs and into my feet. I sat, trying to work out what would happen next. Was this it? Was I getting better? I stood up only to find that my legs were very shaky, the buzzing made me feel as if I was moving continuously. I sat down. No difference; I still seemed to be moving. I waited a while, but nothing changed. Shaky legs and internal vibrations were my new companions.

My neighbours knew I had time on my hands and, in what was fast becoming a daily ritual, I joined them for a cup of tea. I liked visiting them; they would chat away, telling me about their day, recounting stories about their family, involving me in their world. One day my neighbour suggested I attend an afternoon crafting class with her. Did I know how to tat? How to tat? I was lucky I knew what it was. The wife of my school history teacher had tatted, but despite it being an old enduring craft of intricate knotwork, it wasn't practised much where I grew up.

Although I had agreed to join the session, I'd asked my neighbour not to tell people what had happened to me. I was embarrassed. However, I was content for my tatting instructress to be told that I was off work and experiencing anxiety. I watched as she took a small plastic weaving shuttle, with crochet thread wound around it. She then arranged the fingers of her left hand and circled the thread around them before demonstrating how to make stitches on the circle using the shuttle in her right hand. It was like magic. I couldn't follow how she'd done it, but soon I was trying to mimic her with my own shuttle and thread. Although I'd wanted to meet people and had acknowledged the other group members, I interacted only with my tutor.

I had to be shown time and again how to make the stitches, and I had to concentrate; there was so much to remember to get the positioning and rhythm correct. I made mistakes—all picked out with a handy, sharp implement drawn from a craft bag. As I worked, I noticed that the tightness in my chest, the heavy weight bearing down on me, had eased. I had been busy following instructions and watching demonstrations and hadn't thought about how I was feeling. It was so nice to feel lighter, more normal. Maybe the horrible buzzing feeling had left me because I had been concentrating on something else. Maybe the gentle back-and-forth rhythm of tatting was calming. Maybe it had hidden health benefits. I pondered this as the session ended and I took the shuttle and thread to keep practising. As I walked with my neighbour to the car, I felt the familiar heaviness descend on my chest. I realised that the tatting relief had been temporary. But there had been relief.

I was keen to tell my husband about my afternoon craft session. He was barely through the door before I was showing off my new tatting skills, demonstrating what I had learned. Later I sat with plastic knitting needles and some deep-coloured fluffy mohair wool, knitting a scarf. I dropped stitches but used the technique Mum had shown me to pick them up and continue with the pattern. As I dropped another stitch, I noticed a hole a few rows beneath. It seemed to grow, stitch after stitch unfurling. I'd never seen the unravelling effect of dropped stitches right before my very eyes. Although I only intended to pull out a few rows, I discovered how difficult it was to pick up the stitches again. With growing frustration, I pulled everything out and was left with a rather untidy ball of wool.

Rather than start again, I opted to practise tatting and picked up the shuttle and thread. Everything I had learned earlier and shown my husband seemed to have disappeared from my head. I became frustrated and annoyed, where hours earlier I'd felt calm. I tried again but wasn't sure if I was holding my hands and the thread correctly. The movements that had seemed so elegantly simple now seemed impossible. Why couldn't I simply repeat what I had done earlier?

Putting on my shoes, I left to see our neighbour. I had to see her; I had to find out what I was doing wrong. I had to make sure I could tat. It was almost 10 pm, well beyond unsolicited visiting time my husband said, but seeing there was no stopping me, he quickly followed. My neighbour was in the sitting room in her night attire, plainly ready for bed, but I quickly told her my problem. Gently, she suggested I sit on the floor in front of her and she corrected the positioning of my fingers and confirmed how to move the shuttle. After a few tries, I remembered what I needed to do. Making a quiet apology, my husband led me back to our house, telling me it was time for bed.

The next day my husband reminded me how much I enjoyed reading and suggested I join the local library. I hadn't read a book, newspaper, article or words for around two months. I had no interest. I had watched Mum and Dad read their daily newspapers over breakfast but hadn't joined in. Since becoming ill, I hadn't tried, been tempted or wanted to read.

However, I needed things to do, so here I stood outside the library in our small market-town trying to work out how to get in. I followed some people who walked with purpose inside. They seemed to know what they were doing. I passed the issue desk and wandered further, the tall shelves surrounding me in a menacing way. Books were everywhere. Instead of comforting me, drawing me in, they overwhelmed me. I had to leave.

The following day I tried again and managed to ask a staff member how to join. Soon I was in possession of a plastic bar-coded card, the key to happy book reading. I wandered along the shelves; there were just so many books. How did I choose? How did people know what to read? It was like I'd never been in a library before, my search aimless. After looking at several books, I decided just to pick one. I took a heavy hardback, went to the issue desk and watched the staff member stamp the return date.

Outside again I went to my small car and decided to go to the local leisure centre. My doctor had suggested exercise, and I needed somewhere closer than the gym I used to visit. Driving over was uncomfortable; my legs were shaking, and I was gripping the steering wheel tightly. In the car park I chose a spot away from other cars. As I got out, I noticed I had taken up two bays. I thought about re-parking, but I couldn't work out how to manoeuvre the car within the lines of one bay, so I left it. At the front desk I explained I was interested in using the gym. All the time it seemed as if someone else was doing this and I was observing. I wasn't really there.

I was shown the gym and told about the available group classes. I looked around and then, remembering the doctor had suggested badminton, asked where I could play badminton. It never occurred to me that I would need someone to play with. The woman showing me round looked surprised and said she had understood I wanted to use the gym, but we could look at the courts. I listened while she told me about membership rates, but I didn't absorb anything. As we left the badminton courts, I explained I wanted to discuss membership with my husband. I didn't feel I could commit to joining but wasn't sure how to phrase this, so it didn't seem as if I'd wasted her time. I went back to my badly parked car before making my way home.

Despite attempting to build a routine, my days seemed empty. They stretched ahead of me. Every morning I asked myself if I would feel better today. Every day, I felt the same nothingness. Emptiness. Vacantness. I found it hard to get through the day; I couldn't identify things to do and had no interest in trying new things. Each evening after visiting my neighbours, I would be perched on the edge of the sofa, arms tight around me, rocking gently backwards and forwards, willing my husband to come home.

I didn't seem to be making progress, but at my next appointment the doctor reviewed the medication I was taking. She continued the anti-depressants but changed the sleeping tablets because I found them horrible. Sure, they made me sleep, but I loathed the taste. She asked again if I had a project to work on and, when I said no, suggested it was OK to watch television all day. She reassured me things would get better. As I walked home after taking my new prescription to the chemist, I felt confident. I *would* get better. After all, the doctor knew more than I did. But with each step my confidence diminished, and my mind filled with negative thoughts about my future life.

My feelings of inadequacy weren't helped by trying to create a thought diary for the next session with the counsellor. What should I record? How should I record it? I just didn't know. I'd write nothing for a few days, then force myself to write something just before the appointment. I was 100% anxious, had a strange taste in my mouth and my body buzzed like I was being supplied by an electrical current. What particular thought or image had brought this on? No idea. I was in a situation I didn't understand, and I had to fight to get myself out of it. That's what people did when they were ill, wasn't it? They fought to get better, with everything they had. And I wanted to get better.

I had a dilemma about my next counselling session. After driving to the leisure centre, I wasn't sure I was safe to drive any more. My legs were shaky, and I wasn't confident about manoeuvring the car so, after talking to my husband, I decided to stop driving for a while. Not a hard decision—I'd never liked it. Transportation and I didn't gel after I outgrew my scooter.

I learned to ride a bike but didn't have the same affinity as with my scooter. I wanted to glide along gently, effortlessly, like my friend and her family. Instead I wobbled and stuttered. Riding my Christmas present (a commuter bike with small wheels), it started to fold up as I crested the humped bridge at the bottom of our road. As my rear-end and my hands met, I managed to jump off before my bike lay in a heap. It was the end of bike riding for me.

Cars weren't much better. Mum and Dad had an orange VW beetle when we were small and, as Mum was a smoker at the time, we drove around in a fog-filled car—my sister and I with our faces pressed against the back-windscreen mouthing 'help, let us out'. I'd nearly fallen out my aunt's car as we drove over some particularly bumpy 'bumps' and was only saved by Mum grabbing hold of my jumper.

It wasn't any better when I learned to drive. Before starting lessons, I'd dreamed I was driving along the High Street in our village. I was approaching the main road and even though I knew the place well, I didn't know how to navigate the junction. It was a vivid dream, and I remembered every detail and the associated feelings of uncertainty, unease and distress.

Although I passed my test, I didn't have many opportunities to drive. This didn't dissuade one of my school colleagues in Germany, who loaned me his car when my parents visited. 'It's an automatic', he said, 'quite simple to drive'. He was right; it was simple. We drove round with all the windows open as an odd smell grew worse as the visit progressed. After returning the car, his wife apologised. Her fresh fish had fallen out before I picked up the car and had begun to rot under the driver's seat.

Still, they were content to loan me the car again when my friend came to stay. We had a wonderful time, zipping through the Bavarian countryside and, after dropping off another friend at an outdoor centre in the middle of nowhere, I re-joined the road. Beginning to speak English with my friend, I noticed a car coming towards us as we entered a forest. I just managed to avoid a head-on collision, jerking the steering wheel and feeling the impact. In German, the driver yelled, 'Are you drunk?' I replied (also in German), 'No, I'm just Scottish.' I had been driving on the wrong side, not him. There then followed the embarrassment of driving to a local police station to report the accident before calling my friends. They were lovely; 'That's what insurance is for', they said, when they came around with a bottle of whisky to commiserate. I couldn't believe I had been so stupid.

So, all in all, stopping driving when I couldn't concentrate and was very shaky seemed a good thing. But I still needed to attend my counselling session. I broached the subject with my neighbours, who were happy to help. As I walked up the path to the counsellor's house, I could hear voices inside. Maybe the counsellor was on the telephone. After ringing the bell and hearing more voices, the counsellor opened the door. 'I'm not expecting you now', she said. I looked at her and said that I'd written down the appointment in my diary. The counsellor repeated, 'I'm not expecting you now', and explained that my appointment was on another day and she had to return inside. I said sorry and, as she closed the door, wondered what to do. I was sure I had written the appointment on the right day and at the right time. How had I got it wrong?

Back on the street, I reached for my diary. Written on that that day was an appointment with the counsellor. Had I got the right time on the wrong day? Or the wrong time on the right day? No, the counsellor had said my appointment was on another day. I'd written down the appointment at the last session when she confirmed it, but obviously wrongly.

I went over our encounter as I walked. 'I'm not expecting you now.' If it had been me, I would have apologised, said there must have been confusion, maybe crossed wires. I'd have taken some responsibility (even if it was misplaced) so the other person didn't feel too bad. But she'd just said, 'I'm not expecting you now'. No sugar-coating, no thinking of me, no apparent consideration of my feelings. I was unfamiliar with handling a situation in this way.

Was this the type of 'I' statement mentioned in 'The Rules of Assertion'? Number 3, on the small card given to me by the Crisis Team when I was with Mum and Dad, read, 'Make clear 'I' statements about how I feel and what I think'. Was that what the counsellor had done? Was my anticipated handling of the situation wrong? She said it in such a straight-faced way, but it was effective. She had said what she needed and returned inside quickly, probably to a client who had written the correct date and time for their appointment!

I reached town, walking through unknown streets, made some purchases and returned home. When my neighbours later asked why I had returned so early, the counsellor's words rang in my head. Somehow, I couldn't admit to my mistake. I still didn't understand how I'd made it and I felt that I'd wasted their time in taking me to the appointment.

Although my husband had explained we were OK financially and encouraged me to concentrate on getting better, I still worried. I'd always worked, never not earned. There was no way I could return to my job. Not when I couldn't think, read or plan. If I couldn't do my job, what would I do? What sort of role instead? I began to worry more and more. How would my husband afford to look after me when I couldn't contribute? What would happen to us? Would we have no money? Would we be able to pay the mortgage? Would we lose our home? We would. If I couldn't work, we wouldn't have enough money. We'd lose the house, my husband would leave me and what would happen to me then? All these thoughts churned through my mind, weighing me down. I couldn't see how things would improve. The very worst would happen. I was going to lose my husband and everything else. I was scared. So, so scared.

I tried to tell my husband about my fears. He repeated that we were OK, we hadn't lived extravagantly and had some savings. I was also doing my bit by finding bargains when shopping! I looked up at him, from my position in his lap, safe in his arms, the only place I really felt safe. I needed that contact. I needed to be held. My husband tried to encourage me, telling me I was the queen of buy-one-get-one-free offers and was also saving money by walking everywhere.

Despite his reassurances, when I was alone, it was all I thought about. How can I make up the financial hit? How can I try to make our situation better? How can I save more money? One night, I scraped out any remaining potato or vegetables before washing the pans. I put the scrapings on a small plate, covered them and put them in the fridge. That became my lunch next day. I was really pleased with myself and scraping the pans became a daily occurrence. It wasn't much to eat, though, and I was continually hungry. One night I hit upon another idea. My husband didn't like broccoli stalks—I could steam them and add the stalks to my left-over lunches. I'd save money and reduce waste at the same time. I didn't tell my husband what I was doing, in case he tried to stop me. I thought he might notice if I returned the stalks (without the florets) to the fridge and start asking questions. So, I hid them at the back of a cupboard, where I stored onions and potatoes. He wouldn't see them there. I was able to keep a broccoli stalk stash to dip into, supplement my meagre lunches and help us financially.

Despite my efforts, I continued to worry about working again. Something inside told me I couldn't return to my previous job. How could I manage others when I couldn't manage myself? A driving job was out because I couldn't drive. That ruled out a whole host of jobs. Coming back from the shops I passed an employment agency, which I hadn't paid attention to before. I stopped to look at adverts in the window, although they were difficult to understand, with lots of unknown technical terms. I didn't seem to have any of the experience needed. What would I do? I couldn't spend my life trying to find bargains. That night I told my husband I'd started to look at jobs, but there were none suitable in the agency I'd passed. He held me tight and reassured me it was too early to think about work. I still had a job, even if a return to it seemed impossible. He explained I wouldn't be qualified for jobs in that agency window anyway. It was a recruitment firm for the technical sector, not a general recruitment firm. How had I not realised? How didn't I notice as I read the adverts? My husband cuddled me and told me to keep concentrating on finding cheap deals. We would look at my work situation when I was better.

One morning as I ate breakfast while watching television, I noticed a man pass the semi-detached house opposite, then return a few minutes later. Although I didn't recognise him, I didn't think too much about it until I saw him on the roof of the garage, straddling its apex. Something wasn't right. Maybe I should call the police?

I walked to and fro, trying to work out what to say. Maybe it was entirely innocent? I wasn't sure what to do. Ordinarily I would have been decisive and called the police for them to work out the situation. Now I was hesitant, unsure, uncertain. Should I call? Should I not call? What would I say? As I stood in my own internal dilemma, I realised I could see only the man's feet as he slithered through the bathroom window. I'd like to say I sprang into action, but I fumbled around for my phone, then tried to work out how to call for help. Nothing was instinctive, nothing was easy, everything required effort beyond that which I was used to. When my call was answered, I haltingly gave details of my location and what I'd seen—a man looking around a house, straddling the garage roof and disappearing into the bathroom head-first. The responder explained another neighbour had reported a potential burglary. Oh. Is that what I should have said? Was it simply, 'Hello, I'd like to report a possible burglary'?

I finished the call, relieved someone else had taken the initiative, as I couldn't be relied upon. I left the house as a police car sped around the corner before two policemen darted out. One knocked on the front door while the other went around the back. After further knocking, the door opened, and the man stood there half-dressed. After a brief conversation, with the man bringing some documentation to show the policemen, they got in their car and left. It appeared the man lived in the house after all! At least he could be reassured he lived in an area where the neighbours looked out for each other, I thought.

This time I was at the counsellor's on the correct day as expected. She asked me about the recommended book on overcoming anxiety. I explained my husband had ordered it online, but it had left me feeling unable to cope. In truth, I had been overwhelmed and panicked. I hadn't read much since I left work and didn't feel any inclination to read. I'd dipped into the book, flicked the pages, read a few lines but just couldn't do more. It wasn't just the subject matter; I found it hard to look at the words on the pages. Did I tell the counsellor this? No. Did I explain that I felt overwhelmed by her request to read and understand the book? Of course not. Did I own up that I hadn't read the book? Nope. She was disappointed that the book had overwhelmed me. A cue for me to explain that I hadn't read anything in months. Nothing said. Flying had shown that I could get over anxiety, she said; I might not like it much, but my palms didn't sweat as they used to. I would overcome my anxiety.

We discussed my attempts at the thought diary. A simple thing like picking up my work bag led me to think I'd never work again. Watching a program on television where someone was doing their job made me think I couldn't do mine. Everyone else seemed able to do theirs. Why not me? I had difficulty swallowing, a strong taste in my mouth, my chest felt tight, and I trembled constantly. We talked about these physical symptoms of anxiety and my fears that my husband wouldn't want to be with me, because I wasn't capable any longer. The appointment seemed to be over in a flash and we were soon arranging a follow-up appointment, with me taking great care to enter it on the correct date in my diary!

Despite the counselling sessions, I didn't think I was getting better. I was unable to concentrate, remember or co-ordinate things. I wanted to be well again. To me, 'well' meant going to work and not taking tablets any longer. I wanted my work routine, to meet colleagues, review, plan, organise and manage. I just wanted my life back. I was fed up with being confused, uncertain, hopeless. I was fed up with being on my own most of the time. My husband had to work. My lovely neighbours were happy to open their home to me, but I couldn't spend every minute of every day with them. And I felt like I needed that. I needed constant attention, constant reassurance, constant support. Safe in my husband's arms one night, I explained this to him. He suggested I should make a short trip to my family, to celebrate my mum's upcoming birthday. It would be good for me to be among people again, rather than alone at home. I agreed. I had tried to work out things to do, but I needed someone to tell me.

Although I'd travelled by train and tube regularly, this journey was familiar but new at the same time. Instead of the relaxed (usually sleeping!) me, I was tense and observant. Going to the tube was odd. It wasn't rush hour and people moved in an unhurried fashion; they didn't follow the direct routes of commuters, and their suitcases tripped people up.

Disembarking at King's Cross, I saw 'delayed' on the board against numerous services. An announcement confirmed there was snow on the east-coast line. I stood by a pillar, bag at my feet, watching as people went by. The minutes passed and delays changed to cancellations. What if my train was cancelled? I had to get to my family. I had to. I didn't know what I would do if I had to spend more time on my own. I needed them to fill my time and thoughts with anything other than the confusion, blackness and bleakness I was living with. Amongst the delays and the cancellations, my train was announced. The journey was uneventful although we travelled through sleet and deepening snow as we progressed north. I could see flakes fall underneath the yellow streetlights of small villages. I became more anxious. What if we got stuck? What if I couldn't get home because of snow? The carriage became quieter, chatter reduced, as if everyone was holding their breath, hoping they'd reach their destination.

We were here! We crossed the river, curved round the track and stopped. I saw Mum and Dad at the far end of the platform, talking to some people. We rushed towards each other and hugged before Mum took my arm and steered me to the car. It was a quiet journey home, all of us aware of the heavy falling snow, of the need to get back safely. There were sighs of relief when we saw the lights of our village.

I'd packed lightly for this trip. I was only staying the weekend. Next morning, Mum looked at my trainers and decided I needed boots. She and my sister had purchased waterproof, insulated zip-up boots, so we went to a local shoe shop to buy a pair for me. I was worried about spending money. I wasn't working. However, Mum wouldn't take no for an answer and declared them an early Christmas present.

Soon I was wearing snow boots, the last pair in the shop! As we walked to stock up on supplies, we met someone I remembered vaguely from school. I didn't really know her as she was older than me, but Mum knew her well. I stood stiffly in the snow, wondering if she could tell I was ill. What would she think? I felt unable to take part in the conversation. I didn't know what to say or how to act. I became tenser, the longer we stood there. Mum slipped her arm round my waist, drawing me closer. Almost as if she knew how alone and uncomfortable I felt, watching a conversation take place without hope of joining in.

Finally, they said their goodbyes and I tried to smile as Mum and I continued on our way.

Next morning, I could hear faint voices downstairs. Nothing else. Silence. No traffic. No birds. Nothing. I was waking up to the soft quietness that heralds heavy snow. Mum came to open the curtains, telling me we had had a big dump of snow. Looking out there was only white with a grey, ominous sky above. The garden was under inches of snow, tree branches boughed down with the weight. Shadowy outlines hid what lay below. More snow was forecast. How lucky I'd been to get the last pair of boots, said Mum as she left the room.

I love the softness of snow, the stillness as it falls, the muffled sounds and the beauty of everything covered in white. But snow has its downsides. My sister arrived early one evening, distraught, because she'd lost her purse and hoped she'd find it at Mum and Dad's. Faint hope in the house where visitors were greeted with the words, 'Hello, lovely to see you, let me clear a chair'. It wasn't a surprise that, despite our search, we couldn't find it.

Our search became a needle-in-a-haystack job, when my sister admitted she'd gone out on a walk to take photos in the snow. How on earth would we find it? Before Dad and I tried to retrace her steps (difficult since the falling snow practically covered them as soon as they were made!) I suggested we explore my sister's house again. I remembered the book my counsellor had recommended. Since our last appointment I'd dipped into it some more and one thing had stuck. When people lose something, they usually overlook it. The anxiety of losing it means they don't search carefully and methodically. When they can't find it, they become more frantic and less thorough. That's why someone else usually finds the item in a place that has been searched already. My sister insisted her purse wasn't there and we should hunt for it outside before more snow fell; however, I explained that two new pairs of eyes might be helpful, and she relented.

Dad and I looked through her house—the kitchen, the living room, the bedroom, still nothing. Just before leaving, I opened her living room curtains to see if snow was still falling. There, on the wide window shelf was my sister's purse! It had been there all along. My sister had closed the curtains before realising her purse was missing. We congratulated each other that we didn't need to search for it in deep snow, and I reflected that although I had felt overwhelmed by it, I had learned a valuable lesson from the recommended book.

Although I had planned to spend only a few days with Mum and Dad, the bad weather meant otherwise. Snow continued to fall and soon we were blocked in. A handy village barometer for travel is whether the local bus service is running; it tells us if the roads to the north, south and east are passable. The winter of 2010 was testing with heavy snowfall and the buses stopped running.

One advantage of being stranded was that I was with people, rather than at home on my own. However, it meant I was physically contained. I found it hard to deal with this on top of the mental confinement I was experiencing. I felt anxious about everything. I phoned my doctor's surgery to explain I couldn't attend my scheduled appointment the next day. I felt stuck. Caged. Physically and mentally trapped. I went to lie down, to try to relax. As I lay, I remembered the counsellor encouraging me to challenge my thoughts. But I couldn't challenge the snowdrifts outside, which kept me there. Another suggestion had been to visualise taking unwelcome or negative thoughts to an imaginary dustbin and leaving them there. As I tried to breathe deeply, I remembered the old, rusty-red, round bin that we threw ashes from the fire in. I pictured myself opening the heavy lid and thoughts tumbling out of my head. The phone rang, interrupting my thought-trashing. It was my doctor, who listened to how anxious, fretful and trapped I felt and suggested I increase the nightly sleeping tablets and take some diazepam. Mum checked with me after I finished the call and watched as I took the medication, as directed.

With no fresh supplies coming into the village, what would we eat? Mum seemed remarkably unconcerned, reminding me that we had a freezer full of food in the coalhouse, accessed outside from the back garden. I know, it's a strange place to have it, but Mum thoroughly cleaned the coalhouse after their central heating was installed and situated a large freezer there.

She explained there was meat in the freezer, potatoes in paper sacks under the stairs, a store cupboard filled with baking ingredients and homemade jam in a cupboard in my bedroom. The meat for that evening's meal was chosen and Dad dispatched to get it. Outside the kitchen window a snowy, icy scene lay before us. With no interruption from Dad. We waited. Still nothing. Dad came back and delivered a blow to dinner plans—the back door wouldn't open.

We couldn't get to the freezer and the food it contained. Mum, of course, was sure she could open it and set off to the back door with Dad in tow. After a heated discussion and some pulling and tugging, they returned. The wooden door had swollen due to the snow and was now frozen solid. A change of plan for our meal then, as Mum made savoury bread pudding with bacon, onions, bread, cheese, eggs and milk. As she cooked, she said in a very definite tone that as soon as the bad weather had passed, the door would be replaced.

Another advantage of being cut off was spending more time with Gran. We chatted for a while before she suggested I crochet something to keep my hands occupied. I explained I didn't know how to crochet. She stared in disbelief. How was it possible I'd never learned? I reminded her she had once tried to teach me, but I couldn't do it. Why hadn't I tried again? I told Gran I liked knitting and was content with that. There was no stopping her, though; now would be a good time to learn, she declared!

Soon we both had crochet hooks and balls of wool, and Gran showed me how to make a slipknot. So far, so good! Then she showed me how to hold the wool, winding it through some fingers in her left hand. I tried to mimic her but couldn't, so I moved from my seated position and perched on the arm of her chair. Maybe if I watched from behind, it would be easier to understand. Clumsily I tried to copy the way she held the wool, watching as a stitch appeared, with one beneath it. How did she do that? Hesitantly I tried to copy, but she worked instinctively, and I was lost.

As Gran made a chain, stitch after stitch appearing, she exhorted me to 'try, try and try again'. Robert the Bruce, a Scottish king in the fourteenth century, hid in a cave for three months after a battle defeat. He was inspired by a spider trying to build a web. Although it fell down repeatedly, it kept on trying until finally it was successful. Gran's favourite saying was 'try, try and try again', and her dogged determination enabled her to master any craft she turned her hand to. Her shelves were filled with books about specialist stitches, elaborate embroidery, fancy floral art and complicated crafts.

When Gran's chain resembled the length of a rope, she showed me how to crochet into the (five) stitches I had made. Her hands moved with co-ordinated ease. How did she do it? It looked easy, but I fumbled around, becoming thoroughly frustrated. This just eluded me. Even though Gran bent over me, trying to take my hands to guide the movements, I couldn't do it. I sensed she was also frustrated, but I wasn't prepared for her comment, 'Alison, even the handicapped can crochet'. I left the room, muttering about coffee, the crochet hook hanging off a chair arm, not to be picked up again. I would stick to knitting!

One morning I sensed a certain frostiness at breakfast. None of the usual jokey quips or teasing. No nicknames. Mum wasn't reading aloud articles from the newspaper. When I asked how cold it was, the reason became evident. Mum had bought Dad a thermometer a few weeks before. He had asked why. She excitedly said he could check the temperature in winter whenever he wanted (even though he could just check the usual way—by going outside!). The thermometer was on the bathroom windowsill. Mum had congratulated herself on this perfect location, now that the back door was frozen solid. However, Dad had knocked it to the ground below when he was feeding the birds out the window.

We couldn't go out to retrieve it. Operation Temperature Watch could only be resumed via the bathroom window. Completing my morning ablutions, I assessed the possibilities. The window was long and narrow, and it opened outwards on a hinged frame. If I climbed out, I couldn't get back in. Could I reach the thermometer by leaning out the window? No, my arms weren't long enough. What if Mum and Dad held my feet and I dangled out the window, head-first?

Armed with a potential solution, I talked them into my plan and climbed on a stool. I clambered through the window and, after each had hold of a foot, I began to hand-walk down the wall outside. The ground was nearing. White, sprinkled with seed. Sultanas. Half an apple. All for the birds. Now at full capacity, Mum reminding me to be careful, I moved forward. The windowsill pressed on my legs. My head started to feel fuzzy. I was determined to reach the thermometer. I wanted to prove I could still do something. I inched my fingers forward until they curled around it. Success! I struggled to reverse the manoeuvres, thrusting the thermometer towards Dad for safety while they pulled me back inside.

I was bruised and a bit disorientated from being upside down, but our actions resulted in the resumption of breakfast pleasantries.

I'd brought the relaxation CD with me, and although the woman's voice was comforting, I was far from relaxed. I lay stiff as a board on my bed, frustrated I couldn't find respite from the electricity surging through my body. I went downstairs, holding on to the bannister for dear life. Mum was in the kitchen and I told her of my frustration. She tried to encourage me, reassure me all would be well.

She suggested we try the breathing exercises together. My sister came in just then, shaking snow off her boots, and soon the three of us were lying on blankets at odd angles on the living room floor. With my head close to an armchair, I listened as Mum quietly intoned, 'Breathe in, hold and breathe out' repeatedly. I glanced at my sister, whose head was perilously close to the hearth. She was breathing slow, deep breaths, her stomach gradually filling before subsiding. Bemused that she breathed so fully and peacefully, I sat up. How could she do that? Mum encouraged me to lie down and continue, but I wanted to know. My sister turned her head without raising it and explained she'd practised slowing her breathing.

I flopped back on my blanket, frustration mounting. I couldn't do what my sister could. My raspy breaths went in and out, in and out, in and out. A short, staccato rhythm. I watched as her stomach rose as she breathed in, then lowered as she exhaled—almost mocking my feeble efforts! I continued trying to breathe deeply, looking at Mum, whose head was close to the window, her feet towards me. Mum's stomach dipped as she breathed in and extended as she breathed out. I turned. My sister's stomach extended as she breathed in and dipped as she breathed out; the opposite to Mum.

Confused and becoming more frantic, I asked them which was the right way. I sat up again, looking from one to the other. 'I'm not breathing correctly', I cried. Still lying down, they turned their heads to me in wonderment. I quickly explained their breathing differences. How could I breathe calmly, when I didn't know how to do it correctly? Should my stomach extend or dip when I breathed in? Which one was it? Which one was right? Mum sat up and told me to stop worrying, but I began to wail. I didn't know how to breathe properly! As Mum left to finish the evening meal preparations, she told me that, of course, I knew how to breathe. After all, I'd been doing it for over forty years.

I was still in Scotland. Snow was still falling. Nothing moved. I'd arrived ten days ago for a short visit, had missed a doctor's appointment at home and was utterly frustrated. Incapable of much mental activity, now I couldn't do much physically. The feeling of being trapped overwhelmed me as the days and hours passed. Mum suggested I join them at church, explaining it would be nice to see people. I hadn't accompanied them during my last stay. I hadn't wanted to be out in public; I didn't want to try to explain what was happening. However, Mum convinced me and soon we were walking along the road, alongside piled-high-with-snow pavements. As we turned up the hill, I saw the church, looking as it always did, a constant in the chaos I was living, members of the congregation entering through the large doors.

My interactions with people were limited—taking a hymn book and donating to the collection—and I was able to sit, listen and sing. The end of the service, when everyone had coffee in the vestibule, concerned me. Dad, in his role as church beadle, had to attend to some post-worship matters. Mum was involved in at least six different conversations about flower rotas, upcoming communion, delivery of newsletters, et cetera. I stood close to the wall, trying to shrink back into it. Trying not to be noticed. However, someone I knew approached me. We chatted a little and I felt able to say I wasn't doing too well. I was suffering from depression. She sympathised and told me she would pray for my recovery. It was lovely. She was so gentle, quiet and undemanding. There were no questions. We said our goodbyes as Mum and Dad approached. Mum had been right; it had been good to go out.

Although Mum had been sure we had enough food in the store-cupboard, she became concerned about running out. There weren't enough vegetables for soup, a sure sign of trouble. I asked if she had done an online grocery shop before. My reward? A raised eyebrow and a look that read, 'Who do you think I am?' I was sceptical about online grocery shopping, following an observation one Christmas Eve in a supermarket. As we navigated around the vegetable displays, I overheard two staff members discuss an online shopping order. It read one brussels sprout. After discussion, a solitary brussels sprout was placed in the trolley. I had visions of the recipient announcing, in the style of Margo

Leadbetter in a yuletide edition of *The Good Life*, 'Christmas has not been delivered to this house!' Maybe things had improved, but I wasn't sure an order would turn up, given the weather.

Online shopping was the only way to acquire onions and carrots, decided Mum. She asked me to get on with it and so I found the registration page of the nearest large supermarket. I was slow and deliberate. This had to be right. The stomachs of our family depended on it. I entered our name and address and the site opened. After ordering considerably more than onions and carrots, we chose a late afternoon delivery slot and made payment.

Mum started to celebrate. I reminded her we didn't know if the driver could make the delivery. If he did, he might not bring everything. Our delivery slot passed. Nothing. I was downcast. I had probably done something wrong. Mum told me it was more likely just a delay, cursed the weather for freezing the door and tried to make something out of nothing to eat. Just after 9 pm, the delivery man arrived. He had made it! Apologising for his lateness, he said the roads were terrible. Mum, spying a carrot at the top of a bag, was all hospitality and gratitude, offering him hot drinks and something to eat. The driver had another delivery, so we took the bags and wished him a safe journey. We received most of the delivery, and I felt quite proud my first such online foray had helped restock the pantry.

Mum reassured me I was getting better. I had gone to church, I'd been determined to retrieve the fallen thermometer, and I'd done an online shop. I couldn't have done these things a few weeks before. But, although lovely that she had such faith, I felt totally unlike myself. Dark thoughts consumed my days. I felt incapable. When would I be better? Mum had no answer. Neither of us knew. But she was certain I would get better. I wished I had a broken arm or leg. Something physically obvious, because we knew that breaks healed. We could guess how long it would take. We knew people who had broken limbs and their recovery was our reference point. But, with this, we just didn't know. And I was finding that not knowing was unbearable.

Dad had seen a bus. The buses were running! So, the roads must be passable. If the roads were passable, I could go home. If I were home, I could see my doctor. If I saw my doctor, I would get well. All these thoughts entered my head one after the other. I asked when we could set off. Mum suggested caution. There was still a lot of snow; it would be dark soon and we didn't know if trains were travelling south. We should wait until morning. I understood she didn't want to go immediately, but I didn't want to wait. I wandered around the house aimlessly, unable to settle. Why couldn't I get home? Mum suggested I clear the snow and ice around the car. I needed to do something, so I was soon outside with a snow shovel. It was strenuous work, but when finished, I didn't stop. I packed my small bag. I was determined to leave next morning. I was going home. I was going to get better.

Next morning Dad went to warm up the car. It had been stationary for around ten days and was covered in snow and ice. Finally, we're on our way, I thought, standing in my Heidi hat, stamping my snow boot–clad feet to keep warm. Dad tried to get the key in the lock. No joy. It was frozen. He went to boil the kettle to warm the key before continuing his attempts. Soon there was success. Partial success anyway. The passenger door opened. The back doors, the boot and the driver's door remained stuck solid. We worked out a strategy to get in the car through one door. I would go in first to the back seat followed by my bag. Then Dad would climb in, clamber over the gearstick and handbrake (not an easy feat) before Mum took the passenger seat. Some seat adjustments, a few mutterings from Dad (possibly swear words?), seatbelts on and we were off!

Nothing happened. Had Dad warmed up the car? With my insistence we needed to go and frozen locks and doors, we'd overlooked the need to warm up the car. We sat in our cold cocoon, Dad trying to start the car at regular intervals, me willing it to start—to splutter to life. To make a sound, anything. *Just so we could go.* I needed to get home. I couldn't wait. Why wouldn't it start?

Finally, Mum ordered us out. Our breath was steaming up windows that couldn't clear, because we couldn't get the car started. With sighs all round, we began reverse manoeuvres: Mum out, Dad shimmying his way over, the seat moved forward to let me out. We stood in the cold before Mum suggested a hot drink. I was so frustrated. I needed to get home. I had to. At last Dad had the car started, but it was still accessible only through the passenger door. We barrelled out the front door, slamming it as we went. Like a well-rehearsed drill, we bundled ourselves through the car door into position and Dad put the car in gear. This was it. I was going home.

Despite the snow, my journey home went without a hitch. My husband collected me, in my small car, which was better in the snow. Once home he showed me a letter stamped with my employer's name. I didn't want to open it. I knew I had to. I had had no contact with work for over two months, as my manager had been liaising with my husband. With encouragement, I opened the envelope and scanned the contents, before passing it to my husband. I hadn't read it. I didn't want to know what it said. My husband explained I needed to attend a meeting with my employer's Occupational Health doctor. It was scheduled for the following week and was arranged under a formal absence-from-work policy. I panicked when my husband said this. I couldn't think, plan or co-ordinate. How was I expected to discuss what had happened with someone I'd never met? I didn't understand what had happened. How could I explain? Feelings of panic consumed me. I was hot and sweating, my heart beating like it would leap out of my chest. My husband tried to reassure me, explaining the appointment would help me return to work. This was the procedure for people who hadn't been able to work for some time. I listened to what he said, but his words didn't break through the state of agitation that had become my norm.

My husband's students had organised a ball for the following night. We tried to attend their events, to show our support and that their lecturers were human (sort of!). I didn't want to go because I was off work and shouldn't go out socially. But my husband couldn't leave me alone at home. As I tried on a dress, I looked in the mirror. Staring back was a gaunt, grey, emotionless face. I noticed that weight was dropping off me. I was usually quite slim, but standing there, I looked positively skeletal. 'Treasure' could be a new nickname, due to my sunken chest. My collar bones stuck out. My arms looked like they would break if touched. I'd eaten well while I was with Mum and Dad, so why did I look like a stick? The dress, which was usually quite fitted, hung off my frame like curtains. My husband was surprised at my thinness too. I not only felt unwell, I had started to look unwell too. We were collected by friends, and I sat in the car listening to the conversation around me. None of it made sense. I had worked in university administration, I knew and understood the environment. Now everything seemed unfamiliar. I didn't recognise what my husband and our friends were talking about, and I felt even more isolated than before. Why did everyone else understand what was going on?

The feeling of detachment continued throughout the evening. I ate the meal, seated with people I knew well. I had no conversation; I listened but couldn't follow what was being discussed and I struggled to answer when asked how I was. With my agreement, my husband had shared with these colleagues some details of my illness and they treated me gently and with consideration. It didn't help, though. I still felt utterly isolated, confused and concerned. One of my husband's colleagues kindly told me to seek a second opinion if I didn't think I was making the progress I should. I nodded my head, outwardly agreeing. Inwardly, all I could think was, *What sort of progress should I have made?* and *How do I ask for a second opinion?* I was relieved when the night was over and we were heading home.

We went to buy a computer the next day as my husband wanted to connect to the internet from home. As he talked with the sales staff, I wandered the aisles, looking at the computers and laptops. My mind kept spinning round and round. I thought about the letter and the appointment I had to attend for work. My employer would expect me back, I thought, and I wasn't ready. They would terminate my employment because I couldn't do the job. I hadn't contemplated my job being taken away from me, even though I didn't think I could return. And that made me even more frightened. What would I do? How would we live? I searched for my husband. I had to tell him I was going to lose my job. They wouldn't want me when they saw what I had become. How were we going to survive? What would we do? Reaching my husband, I interrupted his conversation, grabbed his arm and frantically told him I was going to lose my job—we shouldn't spend money on a computer. My husband looked embarrassed. Other customers stared. The salesman moved away. I hung on to my husband's arm, pleading with him not to buy a computer until we knew what would happen. We would need the money. I wouldn't be able to work. Electricity was charging through my whole body; I was shaking as I tried to express my fears. My husband took hold of both my arms, looked me straight in the eyes, and told me he was going to buy a computer. He would then take me home and we could talk there. I stood silently while he resumed his conversation and concluded the sale, all while trying to ignore the stares of other customers. I sensed my husband wasn't happy with me. His eyes weren't the gentle, loving ones I was used to, but stormy and hard. He joined me, took my hand and led me out the shop, telling me I needed to take diazepam at home, to calm myself down. Over the last couple of weeks, I had upped my diazepam intake.

Two days later I had a doctor's appointment. I told her about feeling trapped while in Scotland, the horrible thoughts I had and my increasing need to take more diazepam. It had been a horrible weekend. I felt panicked. I felt lost. I felt uncertain. I told her I couldn't go on the way I was. She asked if I had thoughts of harming myself; I told her that I'd promised Mum I wouldn't, but I couldn't continue to live this way. I just couldn't.

The doctor referred me to the local mental health service and told me to expect a call that day, due to the urgency of my situation. At home I tried to find things to do, but I ended up sitting, waiting. Later, a woman called to ask me to attend an appointment in the next town. I explained I didn't trust myself to drive, so I couldn't. Gently, she suggested meeting that afternoon in the town where I lived, somewhere I could walk to. I put on my coat, gloves and hat, ready for the cold December day. Just as I was leaving, my husband's car drew up. He'd cancelled the rest of his meetings to attend the appointment with me. I grasped his hand like I wouldn't let it go.

We met the woman, who introduced herself as an occupational health therapist, and followed her through some corridors to a vacant room. Sitting in a small circle, she asked what had led to my referral. Haltingly, I recounted what had happened, including that I had 'put myself in the river' (the strange wording seemed to be the only appropriate way to describe my actions), how hard it was when there was nothing to do each day and how my feelings of internal isolation had worsened while stuck in Scotland. My husband sat beside me, listening carefully. The therapist asked about medication and whether I would try to harm myself again. I told her about the two different types of prescribed medication, which I didn't think had helped, and that I had promised Mum I would seek help before harming myself. I told her how desperate I felt—the impending cuts at work; the pressure I felt to maintain a good service for customers with reduced budgets; the isolation I felt in my role. I explained I had had a happy upbringing in a loving family and my husband commented that it seemed like an Enid Blyton childhood, with dogs, family picnics, and beach and farm holidays.

As our meeting came to an end, the therapist recommended attending the mental health clinic in the neighbouring town for art, craft and creative writing classes. They would give some structure to my days. I immediately said I couldn't drive there, but she replied she would arrange volunteer drivers for me. Was there anything else? I explained I was due to attend an Occupational Health appointment next day, arranged by my employers. She confirmed I wasn't well enough and should call to cancel the appointment, on her recommendation. I felt relief. Someone else was making the decisions that I couldn't make. The therapist gave me a timetable with the three classes written on separate days and added her telephone number, in case I needed urgent help. As she showed us out, she explained she would call the next day with details of my transport. My husband and I left to go home, with me still gripping his hand tightly.

CHAPTER 5

December 2010-January 2011 – Hope

Every night I would ask my husband to hold me, while I asked him, 'Will I get better? But will I really?' He would cuddle and reassure me and for a few seconds everything would be fine, but then I'd ask him again . . . like I was on a continuous loop. It must have been so draining for him; I'd gone from being an independent, assured person to someone I didn't recognise: clingy, needy, full of doubt.

Probably to get some respite from my continual questioning, my husband started to sing to me the lyrics of a song made well-known by the British comedic duo Morecambe and Wise, 'Positive Thinking':[2] I would sit in his arms while he sang softly, listening to the words as they ran over me, somehow beyond my grasp. I wanted to be well so much and I was trying. I just didn't know how to have positive thoughts.

The occupational therapist had arranged for me to try a one-hour craft session, my first, at the community mental health clinic. I understood deep down that I had to help myself get better. Daunting as it seemed, going along to a class would mean I could meet people in a similar situation. I felt so alone. I needed to find out how others dealt with depression and anxiety. I was told to be ready for collection an hour before the session, because the volunteer driver might have to pick up other patients for their appointments.

I waited, sitting on the edge of the sofa, not sure what sort of car or van to expect. I had my handbag but nothing else. A small car parked outside, and a man got out. He rang the doorbell and, when I answered, checked my name before saying he would take me to my appointment. I got into the passenger seat and, while he turned the car, he double-checked where I was to go. I told him the name of the mental health clinic and the town. He said he wasn't sure where that was. As we drove off, I wondered whether going with him was such a good idea. Then he said he remembered what the building looked like and started describing it. My initial feeling of reassurance began to slip away. He was describing the clinic I had visited the day before—not my intended destination. After some discussion, we worked out the general location of the clinic and I looked at the countryside as we drove for around 15 minutes before reaching it. He dropped me in the car park, telling me to go around the side of the building, to find the entrance.

Doing as he said, I found a locked door with an entry buzzer. I pushed the button, waited for a response and said my name and that I had an appointment. With a loud click, I pushed open the door and entered a small hallway. My first visit to the clinic. Reception was on the left, and I made my way towards it. The receptionist greeted me, asked me to sign in and said I only needed to write my first name and the reason for my appointment. I told her I was there for the craft class and she explained the team member leading the class would collect me a few minutes before its start. I should wait in reception. I picked a seat in the corner, furthest away from the reception desk, facing the door. A coffee table with magazines was in the middle of the floor, but I didn't feel like reading. It was strange. There were words in front of me, but I had no interest in what they said. I looked at the posters on the noticeboards— one said that one in four people would experience depression in their lifetime. Who were they? How did I not know people? Why didn't people talk about it more? Other posters offered support to avoid financial difficulties and reminded patients to keep their appointment times. There were some other people in the waiting room; maybe they would be attending the same class as me.

Every so often, people came from behind a locked door by the reception desk and called out first names. Gradually more and more people left the waiting room until there was only one other man and me. The door opened again and the occupational therapist I had met popped her head through, announcing the craft class. The man got up and started walking through the door, while the occupational therapist greeted me, and I followed her. As we went, she explained she had been assigned to be my care co-ordinator. She showed me round the clinic—

consulting rooms in this corridor, turn to the right, through a locked door, along the corridor, through another locked door, a small kitchen on the right for making tea and coffee, and finally into a different wing of the building. Here there were a few group rooms and the 'safe room'. I looked blankly at my care co-ordinator. Why did I need to know there was a safe in that room? I hadn't brought any valuables with me. Nonetheless she checked the sign on the door and entered the room. I followed and realised, as she talked to me, that I'd been mistaken. The room had comfortable chairs, books and an incomplete jigsaw on the table. No safe in sight. My care co-ordinator explained I could come to this room anytime I wanted. If I felt overwhelmed, or if I needed some space. No one would disturb me, but I could ask for help if I needed it. I nodded to confirm I had understood and followed my care co-ordinator into another room.

The man from the waiting room was sitting at a table and we said a cautious hello to one another. He looked slightly older than me. Glue, old Christmas cards, envelopes, card, ribbons and other craft items were on the table. Today's class would be making Christmas cards. When the scissors were brought out, I noticed they were round-ended, like the type you give to children. Looking at them, it struck me that we weren't allowed to have sharp objects.

I thought we might talk, but silence reigned as I struggled to make cards. I sifted through the old Christmas cards; there was a large gold crown with three green diamond shapes purporting to be jewels. I started to cut it out, my fingers unfamiliar with the scissors. Progress was awkward. Reaching for a glue stick, I stuck the crown on a piece of yellow card. Taking some ribbon, I cut a length to border the bottom of the card. Carefully I stuck it down. I didn't notice the ribbon wasn't straight and overlapped the crown slightly. I looked for other things to adorn my card—a red bell and a cut-out cartoon Santa with a sleigh of presents. I was done. Let's just say Hallmark need have no concerns about me muscling in on the card market. With time left and still no conversation, I embarked on card number two. I chose a pale-yellow card for the base and cut out a purple bauble, a green present, a blue robin and a green Christmas pudding drawn in a cartoon style. Applying some glue, I stuck them haphazardly on the card and, finding 'Merry Christmas' in blue lettering on a white background, cut this out too and stuck it down. Phew, two done. Time was almost up and so I got my things together and headed back to reception. The class hadn't been what I thought it would be. Although I'd been told it was a craft class, I suppose I'd pictured a situation where we'd discuss our experiences and help each other while doing it. Still, if these classes gave me something to do to get through the day, I'd continue to come. After making my way through the maze to reception and signing out, I was told my driver was in the car park, ready to take me home. Thankfully, my return journey was less fraught; after all, I knew where I was going this time!

After my husband suggested I develop a routine for the day, I began to try yoga, using a cheap DVD we'd bought on a recent shopping trip. First thing in the morning I put it on, retrieved a mat from the cupboard in the sitting room and opened the curtains. A few minutes into the first session, I realised it would be better if passers-by couldn't see me! As I wobbled trying to do Downward Facing Dog, I listened to the instructions to draw back my hips towards my heels, then walk out my hands and press firmly though my palms and breathe. Oh yes, I had to breathe. I flopped back down onto my hands and knees. This was complicated.

Undeterred, I tried to continue. The Triangle looked like a wonderful posture and it was a standing one; surely there couldn't be too many wobbles with it? I followed the instructions, standing with my feet apart, opening and stretching my arms at shoulder height. After manoeuvring my feet into position (although perhaps not the intended one), I leaned to the side over my right leg, lifting my left arm up to the ceiling. Encouraged by the lycra-wearing instructor to gaze up at my left hand, I promptly fell forward in a heap. My triangle was a sprawling mess. I watched as the instructor moved on to the Tree, but as this involved balancing on one leg, I decided to call it quits for the day.

That morning I was going to a creative writing class. After breakfast I realised that I had something to get ready for—so different from previous mornings. I waited until I heard the beeping sound of a vehicle reversing. A minibus, with 'Patient Transport' written on it, drew up to the house and a tall man with black hair, dressed in green overalls got out. When I answered the doorbell, he checked my name and said he would take me to my appointment, just as the previous day's driver had done. He suggested I sit in the passenger seat and I clambered (rather inelegantly) in. Once we had seatbelts on, he introduced himself and started to make conversation as we drove off, saying that he hadn't picked me up before. I explained I had just started going to the mental health clinic. I wasn't sure what his reaction would be, whether he would ask questions. He didn't; he just chatted about his day so far and what was playing on the radio. We soon reached the clinic and he told me he would pick me up after my appointment. I should watch from the reception window for him.

I walked more confidently to the entry and buzzed before being admitted—the loud click of the door was a reassuring sound. I signed in for my class and waited in reception until my care co-ordinator appeared, announcing the creative writing class. I was the only one who stood up and followed her through the labyrinth of corridors to the group rooms, entering one of them. A table with some chairs filled the room, and I sat down staring at the paper and pens on the table.

My care co-ordinator explained the premise of the class: We'd start with a warm-up, just to get us thinking, then she'd give us a topic and we'd spend most of our time on that. Before the end of the session, we'd read out what we'd written to the rest of the group. I looked around me. I was the only one in the group! There was usually at least one other attendee, she said, but he couldn't come that day.

I took some paper as my care co-ordinator explained that we would write about places. As part of the warm-up she asked me to think of somewhere special—my favourite holiday destination, somewhere I'd never been but would like to go and somewhere that I didn't really like. She went off to make tea, while I struggled to write some words. It was strange. Even though I wrote most things on computer, rather than pen and paper, the oddness of words not flowing freely was striking. I had to think hard about the simplest of words, pulling them forth from the recesses of my mind, wrestling with them until I had them down on paper.

When she returned, we discussed what I'd written. My special place was the 'waterside' by the river in the village I'd grown up. There were lovely trees, the sound of the water and the chance to see birds. Even as I read this out, I realised that the night when I wanted all my head-slamming thoughts to stop, I had gone to the waterside, my special place. My favourite holiday destination was Salalah in Oman, because of the beautiful beach, the frankincense trees nearby and because there were lots of camels. I'd like to go to Iceland to see geysers and hot springs, and I didn't particularly like Las Vegas (too glitzy and not really me). Phew. I'd written more words in that short ten minutes than I had in months and I felt tired!

As I drank my tea, my care co-ordinator asked me to write about our holiday in Salalah. I started by explaining we had flown there from Muscat in a small plane, filled with American oil workers and people in Arab dress. We had spent time relaxing by the pool but also explored the area with a local guide. He drove us to the Tomb of Job, which has a continuous flame and is tended to by a local man. As a woman, I had to wear a scarf over my head and shoulders and we both had to remove our shoes. We drove close to the border with Yemen, seeing camels in the desert, and found frankincense trees growing and surviving on rocky hills in intense heat. Our guide showed us how to tap the trees with a stone so that resin came to the surface. It would harden over the next day or so and could then be knocked off, so that it could be burnt. Different men tapped the trees and sold the frankincense commercially. Although we had visited in May, the locals told us that the rains came in September, changing the landscape from desert to a lush, green oasis. Many families came to enjoy cooler temperatures; the hotels were fully booked, and locals rented out their properties. They lived in tents around the town during this period. It was an interesting holiday, finding out about the Omani way of life and comparing it to ours. I finished the piece saying, 'I feel sad that I think I'll never get the chance to see this type of place again'.

When I read that out, my care co-ordinator asked why I thought I'd never travel again. I looked at her. I couldn't do anything unaided. Couldn't drive. Could barely function. How would I ever travel? How could I afford to? We finished the session soon after and even though I felt upset because I'd lost my life as I knew it, I clutched the piece of paper with those words on it to take home to my husband—a demonstration of something I'd done.

For the third time that week, I had something to do. Today was an art class. When my care co-ordinator suggested it, I had explained, 'I'm not very good at art' (thinking back to art classes at school). She replied that the object of attending wasn't to be good at art but to have fun and do whatever I wanted. While I could understand what she meant, it was hard to know *what* I wanted to do. As I followed the class leader into one of the group rooms, I saw a woman who was a bit older than me. She was sitting at one of the tables using felt tips to colour in. No mandalas or intricate designs for her to colour; instead, she was concentrating on a children's colouring-in book. As I looked at her, I thought, *Is this what I've sunk to . . . colouring in?* I didn't want to colour in, but I still didn't know what I wanted to do. Another man arrived for the class. I looked at the paper, paint, felt tip pens and crayons on the table in front of me. The little dishes of solid paint were hollowed out slightly as water on paintbrushes had been rubbed over them. I felt completely out of my depth. What was I doing here? The man to my left had reached for paper and pencils and began line-drawings of birds. The woman continued to colour in. I sat. Maybe there would be conversation? After all, there were three of us in this class, unlike the day before. Their attention was focused on the paper in front of them. Eyes (apart from mine) were down. Foreheads were slightly scrunched in concentration. Looking around, I commented internally on something I had noticed. With no talking, all I knew about my fellow attendees was what I could see. We each had the same grey pallor to our faces.

I reached for paper and green and red felt tip pens and, thinking of the approaching Christmas, began to draw holly leaves with berries. There was no rhyme or reason to how many leaves or berries. No plan for how to lay them out. I just drew without thinking about it. Time passed and soon the paints and pens were being gathered up. I snuck a look at my neighbour's paper—the most beautiful small birds were drawn over his page, in various orientations. How talented he was! Even though we had been quiet for almost an hour, I needed to speak, to tell him I thought his drawings were gorgeous. He gave me the ghost of a smile but didn't reply. Soon our little caravan of three was making its way back to reception, before we each went our separate ways.

The week before Christmas I had the same three classes: craft, creative writing and art. I felt I was developing a routine and somehow the day was easier to overcome with something to do and people to interact with. Leaving the first class that week, someone called my name. I turned around to see a young woman, who introduced herself as the lead mental health support worker. She handed me a card and wished me Happy Christmas. I was taken aback. I'd never met this woman before, but she had a card for me. How nice was that? I thanked her for the opportunity to come to classes and explained I hadn't been doing well before attending the clinic. She told me she knew I didn't have any hope, that I thought I wouldn't get better. So, she and the team had hope for me. They were such simple words but so meaningfully said. They made me feel that the people around me were carrying me. Providing support. Gifting hope as I ventured on.

I told her I just wanted to be back to how I used to be. She looked at me carefully, before telling me I couldn't go back. I would be different after this experience. My life would be enriched. I listened to what she said, but all I heard was that I wouldn't be me again. What would I do if I couldn't be me? At home I waited till my husband returned from work, needing to tell him what I'd found out. In his arms, I slowly shared that I had met the lead mental health worker. I showed him the card she had given me and told him how the staff had hope for me, because they knew I didn't. He listened as I told him I wouldn't be the same again when I got well. I so desperately wanted to be well, but who would I be when I was? Whereas I saw it from a negative viewpoint, my husband was positive. He explained she didn't mean I wouldn't be me. I would be me but with different perspectives. The experience I was having would help me understand others better. I would be able to empathise with people who were having difficulties or struggling, because I would know what it felt like to be so unwell—to be unable to do things and then to get well again. He said that far from not being me, I would be me plus so much more. Hugging me tightly, he said he was going to give me a new nickname: 'Ali Plus'.

Two days before Christmas I had an appointment with a psychiatrist before the creative writing class. That week I had already seen my doctor and attended a craft class. I knew this appointment was important, though. I couldn't continue to feel the way I did. I waited in the now-familiar reception and watched as people entered, signed in and were then collected for their appointment. A man called my name and I left the waiting room to follow him through the locked door. Instead of turning right, to where the group sessions were held, he led me to the left. We walked along a corridor to a consulting room, furnished simply with a table and three chairs. A box of tissues sat on the table.

He motioned me to sit and then introduced himself and his registrar. Although this was my first psychiatric appointment, I knew a little about how the medical world ran, from working with doctors in various roles. Consultants led the appointment and their 'juniors' wrote notes, observed interactions and dictated follow-up letters. The psychiatrist asked me to tell him how I was feeling and explain what had happened.

I had written some notes on a sheet of paper, because I knew I wouldn't be able to remember everything. I told him I would refer to these notes and started by explaining about the pressure I had felt at work and what had happened in Scotland. I continued that the Crisis Team had prescribed temazepam, diazepam and an anti-depressant, which I understood would take four to six weeks to take effect. I told him about the negative thoughts I had started to have about money, job security, the future and my relationship with my husband.

I relayed how I had returned home, where my local doctor had prescribed new anti-depressants and sleeping tablets as well as diazepam. She had also stressed that the medication could take four to six weeks to help me. During this period, the feeling of being permanently 'charged' had started. Electricity seemed to travel down my body and the negative thoughts continued. I told him about seeing a counsellor and that she had explained I needed to get back to a state of relaxation. I said I had been stuck in Scotland in late November/early December due to the heavy snow and I had felt trapped in the situation. As this was the first time we had met, I explained it appeared I could talk quite normally. Although my planning skills were slowly coming back, I was extremely forgetful. I'd go to the wrong cupboard to get something. Would leave things somewhere and then need to try to find them. I couldn't really co-ordinate, mentioning my culinary attempts as examples. I said I couldn't cope with information processing. It was like others were speaking a different language and I continually had to ask questions. Everyone else seemed to understand the rules of the world. I didn't. The previous week I felt I couldn't go on like this; the medication didn't seem to be making any difference. While people told me I would have increasingly good days, I wasn't. Finally, I said I couldn't relax—my body felt permanently on-the-go, particularly my legs, which were continually shaky.

The psychiatrist listened and asked questions occasionally. He was sympathetic when I became upset, and he let me tell him things in the way and order that I wanted to. I reached for a tissue, not because I was crying (tears still hadn't come) but because my nose had begun to run.

I don't remember much more, although a couple of things remain clear. In his quiet, gentle tone, the psychiatrist asked, 'You don't trust your instincts anymore, do you?' I shook my head. I didn't trust anything I did. Or said. I couldn't. Then he said three words which I clung to: 'You're eminently treatable'.

I looked at him, hardly daring to believe I could get better. But he believed it. He explained he was going to prescribe some new medication. Like before, he said it would take some weeks to take effect. Although he thought it would work, he cautioned me that if it didn't, it would take a few weeks to leave my system. Then we'd commence treatment with a different medication. I nodded my head. I understood what he was saying. It could be hit or miss, but his words 'eminently treatable' meant I needed to be patient. Drawing our appointment to a close, the psychiatrist told me there was a chemist attached to the clinic and I should get my new prescription there. He would see me again in two weeks' time and, in the meantime, I should remember that he and the team at the clinic were going to teach me how to get well. He smiled kindly as he told me that I was a pupil again.

After collecting the prescription, I sat in the waiting room for the creative writing class. I was beginning to feel more comfortable there and had started to look through the magazines sitting on the table. I was called through to the group room, where my care co-ordinator explained there would be another attendee. He was running late. When he arrived, we began the warm-up by writing scenarios involving three named items. 'Small green Loch Ness monster abandons water to move to pottery house, surrounded by pine trees and cones', I wrote. 'Duck makes fruit flan and serves it to fellow guests on paper plates with brightly coloured napkins' was another. 'Key to house is hidden in an upturned bucket decorated with liquorice all-sorts, but don't tell the Loch Ness monster, let him look for it.' Phew, creativity returning or not? Our longer exercise was to write about one of the items. I chose the key, using the coalhouse one at Mum and Dad's home as my subject. I started by describing it and compared it to other keys—the Yale one for my front door, my suitcase padlock and my car key with its fob. I confirmed that, to me, the coalhouse key epitomised a real key—large, rusty and worn. I wrote about how the key was always in the lock, weathered and weary, and how, after the British miners' strike in the

1980s, my family had turned to gas. I finished with 'the key is still in the lock, a constant amongst all the change, old, worn, heavy but still doing its job in a new century'. I felt self-conscious reading out my words to someone I didn't know. Would they laugh? Make comments? Would they question me? I'd been told that people in the class were supportive, but I felt exposed and waited to see what would happen once I finished reading aloud. Nothing was said though and we came to the end of the session after my new classmate read out his work.

I sat on the sofa at home and opened the packet of new tablets, to read the patient information leaflet and check on possible side-effects. I stopped at the words 'anti-psychotic'. What? Anti-psychotic? I had been prescribed medication for psychosis? I couldn't work out what that meant. The words scared me. I had become used to the idea I was depressed and anxious, but this seemed such an escalation of my illness: more serious. When my husband came home, I told him about the appointment and that I was being given anti-psychotic medication. He, as usual, focused on the positive. The psychiatrist had said I was 'eminently treatable' and I would get better. He encouraged me to double-check when to take the tablets and, after reading my creative writing class story to him, another nightly tablet-taking regime got underway.

On Christmas Eve I was again picked up and taken to the clinic for the art class, followed by a review with my care co-ordinator. It had been almost two weeks since my referral and we began to discuss a care plan. She explained that the whole team of psychiatrists, nurses, therapists and support workers met each week to consider and discuss the care and progress of patients. They worked out and planned the type of support we received, and this formed the basis of the care plan. We worked through the form: I had my care co-ordinator's contact details and information on whom to call outside office hours or if she was unavailable. We confirmed the psychiatrist and I had discussed my mental health needs and he had explained treatment and prescribed medication. We agreed I would receive care and treatment, suitable occupational activity and employment support.

My care co-ordinator explained I would continue attending the acute day service activity for approximately six weeks and that longer-term well-being support would then be provided. As I was employed, a support worker could attend meetings with my employer to act as an advocate, take notes and ensure I was fully aware of discussions and decisions. An anxiety management course was being arranged for March, and the clinical team thought I should participate. I agreed. I wanted to do anything that might get me back to being me. My care co-ordinator also explained that, in January, we would look at setting up a traffic light system. We would identify things I did and enjoyed when I was well, then look at recognising signs I was becoming unwell. We also discussed talking therapy and whether it would help me explore factors impacting my mood and anxiety levels.

I felt really supported and that I had come quite a long way in two weeks. Things seemed to be happening now. Maybe I could be better? Maybe I could be independent again? Maybe it was possible?

I woke on Christmas Day without the usual joyful anticipation. My head felt fuzzy. My husband and I discussed whether this might be due to my new medication. I opened presents with my husband and mother-in-law, who was staying with us, but I found it hard to show pleasure or enthusiasm.

I helped my husband with Christmas lunch preparations, typically his domain. My role was to act as commis chef, with chief responsibility for vegetable preparation and cooking. Apart from roast potatoes, which fell within my husband's purview too. I carefully peeled potatoes, carrots and parsnips; cleaned and made crosses on brussels sprouts; and slit the skin off the turnip. Or, as my husband would call it, a Swede (because it's yellow). We agree to disagree on this. As the Scottish national dish is haggis, neeps (turnips) and tatties, I maintain turnips are yellow, not white. My husband watched over me, making sure I didn't cut myself, guiding where to put the vegetables and co-ordinating everything.

The day continued but I became aware that something was happening. My head began to clear and, for a period of maybe fifteen or twenty minutes, I no longer had doom-filled thoughts. My head seemed lighter. Happier. Normal. Something I almost couldn't remember. As soon as it came, the clarity seemed to go, but I had had a glimmer of being me again. After not being able to think, then having horrible, negative, painful thoughts, this was a magic respite. No matter what present I might receive in future, nothing will compare to those brief minutes on that Christmas Day. It was the best present ever.

People told me I'd get better. Everyone seemed so sure and confident. Somehow, it didn't matter how often I heard it, I couldn't believe it. A friend (who was a doctor) had given me an amaryllis and written in a card, 'I know it feels like all is darkness and bleak with *no* way out but that is just what it is like inside a bulb in November. Sure enough, Christmas time a beautiful, fragrant flower emerges once again and the same will happen to you and your life, I promise . . . You will find it hard to believe just now, but keep the faith . . . it will get better!' She was right. I didn't find it hard to believe. I found it impossible.

My doctor reassured me other patients of hers had recovered. They hadn't been able to communicate nearly as well as me. As I left her surgery, I'd remind myself of this. Feeling confident. But the confidence left me, always around the same point as I walked down the hill towards home. I'd feel the usual darkness and doubts descend over me, surrounding me.

Maybe if I tried to remind myself about all these people who were so sure, maybe if every time I doubted, I could feel reassured, maybe I needed to hear them telling me over and over again. I decided to write things down. I always felt more comfortable when I could see and read words. On a small piece of paper I named everyone who was trying to help me:

> <my husband> says I will get better, as do Mum, Dad and my sister
> <my psychiatrist> says I am 'eminently treatable'
> <my doctor> says that I will get better and 2011 will be a much better year for me
> <my mental health worker> says I will get better and my life will be enriched by this experience
> <my counsellor> says I am the same person, just clouded by anxiety, which can be controlled
> <my care co-ordinator> says that I will get better and so does <my friend>
> All these people know—I will get better
> And <my husband> loves me very much—I am a pupil and have to be taught by <mental health clinic> staff

I wrote this just after Christmas and kept it in the right-hand side pocket of whatever I wore, ready to pull out whenever I needed reassurance. That was often. Over the coming months, my little piece of paper would become beyond tattered; it would become practically unreadable.

In the first week of January, my care co-ordinator explained I would join a weekly tai chi class. This meant I would attend the clinic four days a week and have a packed schedule. Waiting for the class to begin, I sat in the waiting room looking at the magazines, reading the odd article. Four other people waited, only one of whom I recognised from my first craft class.

We were led to a group room with some chairs and folded-up tables stacked against the wall. My care co-ordinator led the class and encouraged us to take off our shoes and find somewhere in the room to stand, facing her. She explained tai chi was a branch of a Chinese martial art, but that rather than fighting, we should think of its health benefits. The Chinese had practised tai chi for many centuries and it was a slow-motion exercise. She would show us different movements and we should try to copy them, all the time concentrating on our breathing.

Standing before her, she asked us to think about our posture—to stand straight although relaxed, with our tailbones tucked in and our head feeling as if it was suspended by a golden thread. Beginning some movements, she reminded us to breathe deeply and make sure our muscles and joints were relaxed. Rigidity wasn't part of tai chi, she said. As we continued to move, trying our best to emulate her demonstration, she explained that tai chi needed concentration. While we focused on our bodies and the movements we were making, our minds couldn't dwell on things or project into the future. Our attention was on our breathing and movement.

The hour-long session seemed to pass in a flash. The gentle movements could be made by people of any age and this was reflected by our wide-ranging age group. As we lay down to spend a few minutes relaxing at the end of the class, I was overjoyed to find I almost began to doze off. It may have been the tablets I was taking, but after so many frustrating months, the feel of my body as it spread over the floor, my shoulder blades nestling nicely in the carpet (rather than sharply suspending me due to their tension) and my legs and feet falling gently to the sides, was almost delicious! I felt reassured. I could relax again. I marvelled at the power of the simple movements we had been shown. I was disappointed when the class came to an end and we walked back through the corridors to our way out.

I'd seen my doctor twice since being referred to the clinic, so she was aware I had been prescribed different medication and was attending classes. At my last appointment, she noted that I seemed more settled. Two weeks after my first appointment, I was due to see the psychiatrist again and we sat in a different consulting room, the layout of which was like the other, with a table, three chairs and a box of tissues.

We talked about how I was doing, and I explained I'd had a 'normal' (for me) head on Christmas Day for a short period. He said that was encouraging and I should continue with the medication at the dosage level he had prescribed. When asked if anything was worrying me particularly, I explained that my legs continued to shake, uncomfortably so. They buzzed as if electricity was charging through them. The psychiatrist said he thought this would reduce as I continued with the tablets but, in the meantime, I could try tonic water. I looked at him. Really? Horrible tonic water? I wrinkled my nose as he explained it contained quinine, which could be used to treat restless legs. I was sceptical but, as I left the appointment, resolved to buy a bottle on my way home.

That afternoon my manager was due to visit me at home. This, I was told, would be a formal part of the sickness absence procedure, but not a decision-making meeting. I hadn't seen anyone from work since I'd left that day in September. I'd asked that my husband be there too. I was scared about the impression I'd make and didn't want to meet without support.

Between Christmas and New Year we'd visited family friends of my husband. Although I was attending the clinic and meeting people there, I had found it hard to be in a group. I couldn't contribute to the conversation. I had difficulty following who was saying what. I felt very separate from everyone, as if I were outside the window looking in. My husband told me afterwards they were shocked by how ill I was. So how would my manager react? Would he be shocked by the new me too?

My lovely husband welcomed my manager and went to make us tea, while I sat in a chair opposite him. I felt strangely vulnerable and was glad when my husband returned. We chatted and I explained I was receiving specialist psychiatric support and attending the local mental health clinic four times each week. I looked to my husband for reassurance as we talked, aware I hadn't spoken to anyone other than my family and our neighbours about my condition. I felt embarrassed as I admitted that my memory and concentration were poor, and I was unable to co-ordinate properly. I explained I was on new medication and this appeared to be helping. I said I thought I was improving. My husband nodded. My manager explained we'd meet again once I'd attended an appointment with my employer's Occupational Health doctor. They would assess my progress and potential return to work.

After my manager left, I went to sit in my husband's arms, needing the comfort and security I found there. He held me gently, reassured me I'd been fine in the meeting, that I had said things in a coherent way and that I'd been positive about my recovery. I told him I'd been very nervous and, holding me tighter, he said he knew that. I could feel happy I'd met my manager again; we'd discussed work and now I could continue my recovery. I burrowed into his arms as he said this.

Going to four group sessions at the clinic each week meant I met a lot of different drivers. Sometimes I would be collected by patient transport vehicles with one or two ambulance crew, other times by private cars driven by volunteers. At night, I would tell my husband who had picked me up and what we had discussed. The ambulance driver who drove me to my second session became 'my' ambulance driver, almost as if he was my personal driver. As I sat up front with him, he would share his Christmas chocolates and tell me about how he suffered from the cold. He really needed a hat, he said, but it had to be green to match his uniform. He hadn't seen a nice, green hat. I didn't reply but stored this information away for the future.

After the first couple of art classes, I was feeling less apprehensive about painting and drawing. It helped that what I was doing was just for me. Nobody else needed to look at it, although each evening my husband and I discussed what I had done that day and he looked over anything I had created or written.

After looking at trees in a magazine, I decided to try to draw a tree using felt tip pens. I chose a deep brown and drew a thin trunk, which bent to the right slightly. I added six branches, the top two a little thicker than those at the bottom. Turning to the green pens, I selected a dark one and used it to create leaves. They started out resembling oak leaves, but as I continued to draw, they looked more like mini conifer trees hanging from the branches. I used a lighter green to shade the middle of the leaves on the lower branches, noticing that each leaf was at a completely different angle to the next one. No matter. I was making this up as I went along, not faithfully following a photograph. As the session began to wind up, I looked over my slightly wonky, slightly top-heavy tree. Interestingly, I hadn't drawn the ground, so it looked as if it was suspended in mid-air. I hadn't topped it off either, so there were luscious-leaved branches and a bare top. Oh well. I had passed the time working on something, which meant I hadn't thought about my shaky legs.

Before I knew it, it was time for the tai chi class again. I was standing in the room with a couple of other participants as the music started to play quietly. My care co-ordinator was leading the class again and, as we began the soft movements, I could almost feel myself relaxing. We were reminded about our posture, to keep it upright yet gentle, not to hold stiff limbs or fully straighten them as we moved. As we followed, I concentrated on my breathing, noticing how slow and rhythmic it was, how calm and measured. We were told at one stage to focus on our feet. Feel how they touched the floor beneath us, how they spread out, supporting us. Feel how grounded they made us feel. If we felt anxious, my care co-ordinator said, this was something to focus on—the feeling of being grounded. As we copied the slow, deliberate movements of tai chi, I felt they were a balm to my battered mind and body. Helping me to recover. During the final relaxation phase of the session, I thought how good I felt, how calm my mind was, and how my muscles and tendons had loosened. Overall, I thought how beautiful these feelings were.

At another appointment with my counsellor, I updated her on my attendance at the clinic, the medication the psychiatrist had prescribed and the employment support I would receive. We discussed how having some structure or routine in my day was helpful, and I told the counsellor how much I liked routine. Maybe that was why I had loved my job organising exams for doctors from overseas. The consistency of approach appealed to my sense of order. The counsellor acknowledged my liking of routine but suggested it was OK to shake things up a bit, now and then. I considered this. I could see what she meant. I didn't have to do things the same way every time. Maybe I didn't need to co-ordinate pegs when hanging out washing. I could use different coloured pegs on an item, rather than matching ones. 'Shake things up a bit', I repeated. OK, I'd give it a try. The counsellor suggested we postpone the remainder of our allocated sessions until my return to work. After all, I was receiving specialist support. We agreed I would contact her when I returned to work and I left, resolving to find ways in which I could shake things up a bit.

The creative writing class was on Thursdays, and I began to look forward to wrangling with thoughts and putting words down on paper. There were still only two of us in the class, and I was less self-conscious about reading out my work. I was also now awfully familiar with my surroundings and had used the kitchen a few times between classes and appointments with the psychiatrist and care co-ordinator. Feeling bold, one day I offered to make tea or coffee for my classmate before we started our session. He gave me his order and I set off to get drinks for us and the therapist leading the session. Returning a short time later, I placed the mugs carefully on the table, trying to ensure I didn't spill any over the paper we would use for writing.

As usual we began with short exercises and I drank my tea, while I thought and wrote. My fellow writer wasn't drinking his, so I asked if anything was wrong? He replied I'd given him tea instead of coffee and I hadn't added sugar. I looked at him blankly. I was sure I'd made exactly what he asked for. I checked with him again, but it was plain I'd muddled up his order. How? The kitchen was so close to our room. How could I have given him the opposite of what he wanted? I only had to walk a short distance to make it. It seemed like my ears heard one thing and my brain delivered something different. I was disconcerted by getting it so wrong, despite my companion's assurance that it didn't matter. I spent the rest of the class trying to write, while questioning myself about my memory and co-ordination.

In mid-January I was introduced to my employment specialist. We met in the safe room, and she explained her role was to work with me to achieve my employment goals. We talked about my work history, the responsibilities I had held, the role I was absent from and my thoughts about returning to that same role. I explained I hadn't had much direct contact with work but had recently met my manager. An Occupational Health assessment had been scheduled. The employment specialist described how she might be involved in any forthcoming Attendance Management meetings with my employer. With my agreement, she could accompany me to meetings, read the resulting letters and reports with me, and answer any queries or concerns I might have.

After feeling so alone, as if everything was too complicated, so overwhelmed by the thought of a formal process, her suggestion sounded wonderful. I gratefully accepted her help. She explained we would work in partnership and I would be expected to actively engage with her in our meetings. Responsibility for any agreed actions would rest with me. Information about my journey and achievements would be shared confidentially within the mental health teams, but personal data would not be disclosed to any outside organisations without my written consent. She told me I had a right to view any personal data within my files. I felt reassured after she had explained all this and we both signed an agreement documenting these points. And so I had support in another aspect of my life.

The day before I had gone to have my hair cut and highlighted. I had carefully asked the price before making the appointment, even though my husband had been clear that cost didn't matter. He just wanted me to feel good about myself. I had written the date and time of the appointment in my diary together with the cost. However, the receptionist explained I was only booked for a haircut. No highlights. I was confused. Unfortunately, the hairdresser was fully booked, so she only had time to cut my hair. I tried to work out what had gone wrong. I knew I'd asked for highlights. I'd been given the price of highlights. I'd written highlights down in my diary—at the right time on the right day (not wanting a repeat of the counsellor appointment debacle). But I hadn't booked highlights with the hairdresser. I sat in the chair feeling downcast, thinking about how I continued to get things wrong.

As my regular hairdresser had moved, she had recommended another stylist. We introduced ourselves and began the usual consultation about what I wanted, how short, etcetera. After washing my hair, the stylist began to cut and then thin my very thick hair. As she thinned, we talked, and I explained I wasn't able to work because of illness. Although she asked questions, the stylist was gentle, and I didn't feel embarrassed or ashamed about my situation. I told her about not being able to concentrate and making mistakes, using the muddled tea/coffee order from a few days before as an example. I explained I thought I had booked an appointment for highlights and a haircut but had got that wrong too. When we finished, she made an appointment for highlights a couple of days later. It was so lovely of her to be kind, to be gentle and to be concerned to make sure I received the outcome I wanted.

That night, as I showed off my newly shorn head to my husband, I told him about making another mistake. He told me not to worry, even though I was fretting about it. I didn't have to be perfect, he said. I was far from perfect, I replied! He retorted that I was perfect to him. He pointed out the hairdressers might have written down the wrong appointment. However it had happened, everything had worked out. I had shorter, thinner hair and soon I would have highlights. It didn't matter things had gone wrong. As I was perfect to him and mistakes were allowed, he decided to nickname me 'Imperfect Perfect' from then on.

I had decided to take knitting to the craft class—partly because it meant I wouldn't sit there, wondering what to do with paper, glue and pens, but also because I liked knitting. I was working on woollen hats for servicemen. They had to be in camouflage colours and pure wool, rather than acrylic, in case of burns. I'd chosen balls of green and brown and followed a pattern Mum had sent. Classes were usually quiet, not any conversation really, just the sound of things being moved on the table or scissors being picked up and put down. Outside, the birds called as they flew from tree to tree, and there was a distant hum of traffic. It was a peaceful environment, despite the busyness of the individual clinics held elsewhere in the building.

Partway through the class, we heard shouting. Initially, a little sporadic, some way away. However, it got louder and more aggressive. It was so unusual to have any disturbance, none of us knew how to react. We continued, knitting in my case, others painting or drawing, while the shouts got angrier. It was a man, his voice quite deep. He yelled the name of the lead mental health support worker. I couldn't work out whether she was with him or he was shouting her name, so she would go to him. The commotion continued as I noticed our group facilitator quietly pick up the scissors and leave the room. We looked at each other, trying to ignore the anguish of the shouts, not really acknowledging what was happening. It struck me that, while I viewed the clinic as a nice, safe place, where people were helping me to get better, other patients might feel differently. Depending on their circumstances, they might view it as a frightening place, a threatening place. It was a sobering thought as the cries died down and our facilitator returned to say the incident was over. All was good. Silence descended over our room again.

Two weeks after my last session, I was meeting with the psychiatrist and his colleague. We reviewed how I was feeling. I was beginning to feel a bit more confident, a bit more like myself again. I had experienced more of the 'my head' feelings after my first appointment and these were lasting longer each time. He was pleased to hear this and suggested we increase the new medication and decrease one of the others. I accepted this. Even though I had been almost fanatical about not becoming addicted to tablets, I could see this medication was beginning to help me.

The psychiatrist asked if there was anything else I wanted to discuss. I shared with him my concerns about concentration and memory. A few days earlier I had written a shopping list, since I wasn't sure I would remember what we needed. When I reached the store, I realised I'd forgotten to bring it. Although I tried to remember what I'd written, when I returned home and double-checked the list, I had forgotten some things. My psychiatrist told me my memory and concentration would improve; I just needed to be patient. Not my best virtue, I told him! I used to be able to remember things. I didn't need lists. I could reel off what was needed as I walked around the supermarket. What if I couldn't remember things as well as I used to? He had a good memory, the psychiatrist replied, but he wrote things down. He made lists. He didn't try to tax his brain by remembering everything. I should get into the habit of writing lists and not expecting my poor brain to remember all I wrote, said or thought. We laughed as I said I would continue to write lists; I just hoped I started to remember to take them with me!

Although I had been advised not to attend the meeting before Christmas, I now felt able to meet and speak to my employer's Occupational Health doctor. I travelled by train to the appointment and felt a little self-conscious as I waited. What if someone I knew saw me? What would I say? The room used by the doctor was near the main reception in headquarters. I didn't have to walk through the building, but I still felt concerned in case colleagues passed by.

My manager had sent me a copy of the referral form. It indicated I had acute anxiety/depression and had been witnessed having difficulty performing mental tasks at work. I might have concerns about job security due to a departmental reorganisation that was to take place. An explanatory paragraph confirmed that our service was to be the subject of a major restructure and I would have a key role in both reviewing and proposing a new structure and ways of working. This would be a stressful time for everyone involved. Advice was needed on when I would be fit to return to work, whether a phased return would be appropriate and when I might be able to resume my full range of duties.

On meeting the doctor, she asked me to explain the background to my absence. I explained my role, the locations I worked and my responsibilities. I told her everything that had led to me being referred to specialist psychiatric support in December. While my thoughts were becoming more rational and I felt my concentration was improving, I didn't feel anywhere close to my normal self.

Although I feared the appointment would be the start of medical termination of my employment, I could now see it was about supporting me back into the workplace. The doctor confirmed I wasn't fit to return and acknowledged I was taking significant doses of medication. With my permission, she would write to my psychiatrist to ask when I might potentially return to work. In any case, a phased return would be needed. She would produce a report for my manager and would send me a copy. I explained I was receiving employment assistance from the mental health clinic and she welcomed this, suggesting I discuss the report with my employment specialist.

I felt relieved after the meeting. Following my early-January meeting with my manager, this had been only my second direct contact with my employer, but I had found it helpful and reassuring. I couldn't have coped with these discussions at an earlier stage, but now I was receiving treatment and seemed to be improving, I felt able to discuss my work situation and, also, consider myself back at work.

A lot of this had to do with the support network around me and the care plan arranged for me. A few days after the Occupational Health meeting, I discussed the report with my employment specialist. I was pleased it summarised what had happened and relieved there was recognition that I wasn't fit to return at that stage. The doctor had arranged to see me again in March, noting she did not expect a return to work before this. I discussed with my employment specialist how helpful I found this, knowing it had been made clear to my employer that I wouldn't be returning for a couple of months. Pressure I hadn't realised I felt fell away from me.

The doctor had been clear in her hope for my full recovery, but one comment caused me to pause. Given the severity of my condition and its longevity, the doctor expected employment legislation relating to disability would be relevant to me. Until that point, I don't think I'd accepted how vulnerable I was. I wasn't sure how I felt about that. My employment specialist suggested this was a helpful statement. It reflected the care and support I needed for a serious medical problem, until I recovered. Reading the statement affected me. I thought of my husband, who was always positive. The truth was I hadn't been able to do much for myself. I needed the help and support of a range of services. I was getting better, but there was a way to go before I was capable and independent again. I decided I was OK with this statement, OK with the fact I might need adjustments to get me back to work. I was OK with where I was, because of the help and support I was receiving and the progress I was making.

I was back in the clinic for our weekly creative writing class. There was still only one other participant, but I didn't mind. That week I left him to make his own hot drink. The memory of getting his order completely wrong lingered. We began our warm-up exercises, writing short notes about the seasons, before we ventured on to our longer piece of writing. We were asked to write about our favourite season. As I thought about spring and being amongst nature, I knew exactly what I wanted to write about. The farm where my 'aunt' had lived. After we finished writing, we took it in turns to read:

Walking away from the farm, the sound of the hounds barking in their kennels, down to the burn that runs alongside, I smelt the fresh spring air and looked at the green grass of the hills opposite. Lambing was in full flow, the sheds full of expectant ewes and new mothers with their lambs, the farmer and his son bleary-eyed, taking turns to stay up during the night and then walking the hills during the day to make sure all was well. A collie ran past me on its way to its master and I heard the gentle high-pitched bah-ing of newborn lambs. The fun of bottle-feeding little lambs was on my mind as I sat down by the burn watching the clear water ripple over the stones below. The freshest of air, the gentle babbling of the stream and new life all around, the joy of spring. And as I sat looking at the hills dotted with gorse and bracken, a magical moment as a group of wild hill ponies appeared on the crest of a hill. Beautiful creatures, sturdy, untamed, watching me as I watched them. Some grazed a little, others simply stood and then one by one they were off, cantering into the distance, their manes and tails flying. The burn bubbled and rippled and now a procession of ducks and ducklings came into view—quacking animatedly, following the leader as they came down the track to the pool below me. Gently, effortlessly they glide into the water, the mother ducks guiding their little ones, now no noise, as they feed and swim around. A happy bunch, they bob gently in the water and then, at a chosen time, the leader moves to the edge of the pool and leads the column away to another part of the burn, as I sit and wonder at the magic of nature.

I was happy with what I had written. I felt it conveyed the joy and awe I felt at seeing new animal life. The happiness I found watching nature all around me. After we'd both read our pieces, the facilitator asked if she could take what we'd written to have typed up. She wanted to make the clinic a little brighter by using drawings and writing from the classes to adorn the drab walls. I was surprised she wanted to include my spring story, but it felt nice to have acknowledgement of what we'd written. I felt quite proud that my words might be on display. Hopefully, it would help others, just as coming to the clinic was helping me. That night, without the usual sheets of A4 paper, I told my husband what I'd written and explained he would have to wait for my musings to return, before he could read them himself.

For the next art class, I decided to use some colour. My efforts so far had been green (leaves), brown (branches) and red (holly berries). I wanted to do something brighter and happier. I reached for the watercolour paints and picked blue and red. I had no idea what I was going to do but started to draw boxes with nine squares in them. Then I randomly coloured some of the squares, gradually using more colours—yellow, orange, pink, brown and green. The boxes changed from straight-lined edges to wavy lines as the hollow in each paint colour grew a little larger. Finally, I took a brush and with red paint gently connected the boxes. One to another. No pattern, just making connections. All apart from one box. It sat on its own. Lonely.

My care co-ordinator's words, about having fun and doing whatever I wanted, had stayed with me. I wanted to try things. It was January. Mum was making marmalade and so I decided to make marmalade too. I'd never made it before. My last foray in the preserve department hadn't gone smoothly—I'd nearly burned down the kitchen. The previous summer I'd decided to make strawberry jam. Although I had the jam pan, glass jars and wax lids, the strawberry fields were closed when I went. I bought punnets in the supermarket, but the exercise hadn't started well. I warmed the sugar, chopped the strawberries and sterilised the jars, as I'd seen Mum and Gran do. Then I started to smell burning. Not the sweet smell of sugar burning. I gradually realised, as smoke appeared, that I'd left the oven mitt too close to the gas flame. Although we had some jars of (quite tasty) jam, we also had a charred oven mitt and a smell of acrid smoke in the house. There was a certain degree of risk associated with my new fruity plans.

But really, marmalade-making was big for me because I had chosen to do it—and I was excited. How long since I had felt enthusiasm? Trying something new, wanting to try, and not caring about how it turned out was a magical feeling. I was almost high on the possibility of pectin! I spoke to Mum, wrote down the recipe in my little black book (now filling with soup, savoury and sweet recipes), and bought marmalade oranges, lemons, grapefruit and sugar.

With everything prepared and the fruit cooked in the pressure cooker, I started the fun part—shredding the peel. There was something soothing about this task, making sure the pieces weren't too thick, holding the knife at the correct angle and gradually seeing the pile of shredded peel grow. The kitchen filled with the tangy scent of citrus—so much more refreshing than charred oven glove! Soon the fruit boiled, and I dropped a little pool of marmalade onto a cold saucer, drawing my finger through it to see if it would set. Satisfied, I poured the marmalade into jars and covered them with wax discs as Mum had instructed. There, my first jars of marmalade; I looked on proudly as I took off my apron. No major dramas. No emergency calls to the fire service. Only the sweet smell of sugared fruit.

When he came home that night, my husband pointed out we didn't usually eat marmalade. True. I hadn't thought about or planned what to do with the marmalade. I'd just been so focused on and excited about making it. I gave a jar to my neighbours. They declared it very tasty, although they had to heat it in the microwave to encourage it to leave the jar! I was determined to try again, to see if I could get the consistency right. Despite conversations with Mum and my best intentions and efforts, I produced another batch of thick, resistant marmalade. However, this was the first sign of me being motivated to do something new. It was a success.

CHAPTER 6

January–February 2011 – Green Shoots

I can't tell you when I felt my head was mine again—when the horrible dark thoughts receded, when I was comfortable being alone again. There wasn't a time I could pin-point; things just gradually changed. My head felt like me again, if a little foggy and indistinct, and after my marmalade attempt, I began to try new things. Even though I'd feared the cost of buying a home computer, being connected at home was helpful. I wanted to find other ways to help myself and remembered I'd had cranio-sacral therapy sessions. Mum had told me about a therapist who had moved to the outskirts of the village. After he treated her, she was happy to recommend him. The non-invasive, gentle pressure on her head, neck and back had provided relief. She introduced us on my next visit. My energy levels were low, my arms felt like lead weights and trying to do normal, everyday activities was an effort. At the end of my first session, I could lift my arms easily high above my head. They felt feather-light, such a contrast to when I had walked in. I had also consulted a practitioner when I worked in London and liked the gentleness of the treatment, the ability to let go during the session and the feeling of calm energy that surrounded me afterwards.

Having discussed it with my general practitioner and with the internet at my fingertips, I searched for a local therapist. Finding one in the market town where my employer was based, I telephoned to make an appointment and explained, hesitantly at first, what had happened to me over the previous few months. Although I still wasn't driving, I decided I could travel alone by train to the appointment. I felt I was becoming more independent as I searched for the address and determined the route I would take from the station. Then I checked the train timetable to work out which train would get me there in time. These simple decisions and actions highlighted I was getting better. I couldn't have worked this out several months before.

My first appointment was on a lovely winter morning, sun gradually rising, crisp underfoot, chilly air. Wrapped up in my Heidi hat, gloves, scarf and coat, I set off on my adventure. I was nervous, repeatedly checking I had the map and instructions of where to go, but also a little excited. I was trying something new. Well, new-ish. I was going somewhere . . . semi-new. The train ride was old-hat, but new. Same train company, familiar doors and layout, different direction. South instead of north.

Orientating myself on leaving the station, I walked across cobbled streets to the therapy centre. Inside was light, bright and peaceful. I introduced myself to the receptionist and waited, looking at posters on the wall and flyers on the table. I helped myself to fruit tea, marvelling at my composure, not worried about how easy it would be to dispense from the pot, holding the small pottery cup in my hand. As his last client left, the therapist introduced himself. Inside the treatment room, he first asked about my experience of cranio-sacral therapy and how I had fared over the last few months. I was open with him about my breakdown, telling him how I had become a shell of a person. Needing to be directed from room to room. Told what to do. Unable to think or do things on my own. I told him about the psychiatric care I was receiving, the medication I was taking and the progress I thought I had made over the last few weeks. I explained I wanted to be well again, to be me again, and I was determined to do whatever it took. I thought resuming cranio-sacral therapy might help. He thanked me for telling such a difficult story and said listening to it had been inspirational. He agreed I might be helped by cranio-sacral therapy. He had worked with others who had experienced anxiety and depression.

Showing me to the massage table, he asked me to lie on my back and relax. The remainder of the session seemed to pass quickly, as the therapist held first my head, then my feet and then carefully placed his hands palm-down under my sacrum. It was quiet in the room and I began to feel very relaxed, a feeling which continued as the session wound up. After slowly sitting back up, I explained how I felt—relaxed and a little floaty—before making another appointment and heading home.

In early February, my care co-ordinator arranged an initial assessment for cognitive behavioural therapy (CBT). I didn't really know what that was. She explained it was talking therapy, which would supplement the medication prescribed by the psychiatrist and my participation in group activities. When watching breakfast television, I had heard about mindfulness. Would that be helpful to me too, I asked? My care co-ordinator explained the scientific benefits of mindfulness hadn't yet been demonstrated fully by the Australian clinicians who were leading the field. She continued that the mental health team had agreed CBT might be helpful for me. She would prefer to focus on that.

Having reassured myself I had asked about mindfulness, I decided to see what CBT was like. As I waited in reception to be called through to my appointment, I read my library book. The reception magazines had helped me rediscover my enjoyment of reading. Now I immersed myself in the words and stories contained within the covers. A woman I didn't recognise came through the locked door and called my name. Inside the consulting room we made our introductions. She explained she was aware of the treatment I was receiving for anxiety and depression and we would discuss whether my thoughts had affected my feelings and behaviour. She asked what had led to my referral and so I recounted the difficulties I had faced with the recruitment event, the thoughts that had slammed into my head and my inability to do anything for myself. Asked to tell her more about my work situation, I explained the isolation I had felt. The pressure. Expectations. Responsibility.

Was there anything else that had affected me? I said I tended to think and think, and then think some more, going over and over conversations I'd had or situations I'd been in. I tried to see things from different angles, tried to understand different perspectives, tried to work out what I could or should have said differently. I thought until I really flogged my thoughts to death! I also felt I strived for perfection and found it difficult to accept anything less. I explained my nervousness with driving and that I felt I needed to rehearse and prepare for journeys on my own. At the conclusion, we agreed I would have further sessions to explore things more and discuss strategies that could help.

After the CBT session, I made a cup of tea in the kitchen and ate my lunch in the safe room, while I read my book. I felt very at home and relaxed in the clinic and knew there was a big difference in how I was thinking and acting. The next session was tai chi. I had come to love it—the gentle exercise, the soothing music, the concentration that meant my mind was calm and in the room. My care co-ordinator had explained I would have a couple more sessions before I completed the activity-based programme. I began to wonder if tai chi was something I could continue after leaving the clinic.

I had persevered with my morning routine of yoga in the sitting room (I'd advanced to Warrior 1 and 2 without incident and particularly liked Child's Pose, a resting pose), followed by television with breakfast. One of my regular favourites had been replaced by *Heir Hunters*, which followed investigators trying to track down people who might be entitled to assets from deceased estates. They often visited registration offices to secure birth and death records. Although I had tried to watch an episode, I found it reminded me too much of work. I looked for something else to view.

The drivers arrived regularly to take me to the day's class. Once I was collected by private car and the volunteer told me he had to pick up other passengers. We made our way to three separate houses to collect elderly ladies. It transpired they were friends, thrilled to be having a trip in a car, who had arranged their appointments so they could have lunch at the hospital, turning it into a social occasion. They sat in the back, despite my offering the front seat, commenting on things as they passed, reminiscing about how certain areas used to look and exclaiming over new developments. One remarked she didn't get out much in a car these days, so her trip to the hospital was a treat. I'd never thought much about the limitations older age could bring but, given my current non-driving situation, could understand a little better.

Sometimes we would drive to pick up people, only no one would answer. The drivers would always make sure they rang or knocked twice and left enough time for people to get to the door, but often I didn't have travel companions. Once I was in the patient transport bus with a female driver, who had to navigate very narrow streets to get to a nursing home. It had room for only one vehicle along its drive. She drove alongside the neat lawn punctuated by flower beds, then with a loud toot of the horn, turned a sharp ninety-degree angle. She told me she would have to reverse out as there was nowhere to turn. We parked and I waited while she went inside. After some time, she came out alone. The patient wasn't coming. We duly reversed out, slowly, with beep-beep noises all the way. I was so glad she was driving. I couldn't have reversed my small car the way she reversed her bus.

The conversations I had with drivers and the funny things they said became highlights to be retold to my husband at night. I would sit in his arms while he looked over what I had done at the clinic or listen to what had happened that day. I told him how one of the volunteer drivers had described her friend, who had had numerous operations for arthritis, as being a bit like her old broom—four new heads and three new handles! And how another volunteer driver had invited a couple of friends to watch the Arsenal game on television. They said they were going for high tea first, so she didn't prepare any food. When they arrived, it turned out they'd been at tai chi! She'd had to go to the freezer to get sausage rolls. It was inconsequential but hugely important to me. The drivers were my lifeline to a world I wasn't part of. Their chatter and laughter not only brightened my day but demonstrated love and care. Dropping me off at the clinic, one of the elderly male volunteers told me he didn't have my return journey. I should look for someone else when I was ready to go home. He explained they liked to share out the beautiful ones like me. It was said in such a gentle, caring, non-threatening way. It made me realise I would have brushed off compliments like that in the past. Now I wanted to acknowledge and embrace them. It made me feel good.

The therapist asked me more about my work at my next CBT session. I found myself telling her about how the service had been restructured before I arrived, how unhappy the (largely female) staff seemed and how mistrustful I felt they were of me and each other. They appeared to have lost some benefits in the restructure, and it was clear they had not had an easy time. At the end of my induction week I had had a massive headache. Everything seemed to be a problem—accommodation, staffing, IT infrastructure and the way of working adopted to meet both the ongoing nature of birth and death registrations and the seasonal effect of weddings. I felt expected to solve everything. Soon! Each Tuesday and Thursday, when I found somewhere to work, individual staff members would tell me about their problems with the service. While I felt it important to be approachable and I needed to understand so I could work out how to take things forward, I felt worn down by each comment. The cumulative, negative effect had made me question whether I was good enough for the role. That was before I was told that cuts would need to be made. I felt sandwiched between my managers and the staff, expectation from all sides. I didn't want to let the staff down. But further cuts would have a significant effect on them. I felt I couldn't share this with anyone and so had struggled on.

We discussed how I had begun to take the criticism personally—probably not the intention, but my way of thinking. I felt isolated and unsure of myself. As I went over and over the interactions in my mind, rather than discussing them with my manager, they were always present. Each building on the other. Layer on layer. Magnifying the problems and making them seem insurmountable.

The therapist asked me to tell her more about trying to be perfect. I explained I had high standards and expected things to be done well, otherwise what was the point? I felt I had become overly focused on perfection and would berate myself if I made a simple mistake, a wrong date in a document, for example. She asked if I would tell off a staff member if they made the same mistake. No, I said, I'd point it out to them so they could correct it—after all, everyone makes mistakes. So why was I not allowed to make mistakes? Huh! I couldn't answer. I didn't know. I suppose I just expected I wouldn't make mistakes. As we discussed this, I could hear Mum's voice, reminding me 'to err is human', something written in her school yearbook about a classmate. I hadn't thought of that phrase in years. Discussing the ease with which mistakes were made with the therapist and reflecting started to help me understand the unnecessary pressure and demands I placed on myself. What did it matter if a date was wrong? Just apologise and move on; don't get all wrapped up in it. As we finished the session, I realised I needed to cut myself some slack and not be so hard on myself.

In a session with my psychiatrist we discussed my concerns about driving. I told him about the dream I'd had about it, the interval between passing my test and driving regularly and the crash I had caused in Germany. I explained I couldn't believe I had been so stupid. He countered that it had been an accident. He asked about driving since then and I told him I hadn't driven much, as I commuted to work by train, bus or tube. Since changing jobs and working within the county, I had to drive.

I told him I wanted to drive more, but I was still very scared about it. I didn't like going to new places because I didn't know where to park. I'd even driven reconnaissance missions to unfamiliar places on weekends, often with my husband accompanying me, so I knew where to go alone. If it began to rain while I was at work, I'd start to worry about how to drive home in the rain. Even if it poured in the early morning, I'd feel uneasy and distracted, despite the hours before leaving work. I'd try to work out which route to take and how I would drive in the conditions.

My psychiatrist listened and told me about hearing an interview with Tiger Woods, the golfer. When asked how he got holes-in-one or the ball so close to the hole, he replied that he visualised it. He focused on the ball going in the hole, saying that everything else would work out. Rather than think about the journey, my psychiatrist suggested, I should visualise parking at the end of it. The rest would work itself out. It sounded too good to be true. How could I not think, plan, or plot future journeys? How could I be prepared if something out of the ordinary happened? I needed to concentrate, to be firmly focused, otherwise I might cause another accident. My psychiatrist explained preparation was still needed—I needed to know where to go, which roads to take. I didn't need to imagine the journey, the turns at every junction, the lorries and potential obstacles I might meet. I could focus on my arrival and deal with situations as they developed. He suggested I was wearing myself out mentally before I'd even opened the car door!

I considered what he said. Before going to familiar places, I drove the route in my mind, making sure I knew where the corners, junctions and turn-offs were. What he was suggesting sounded very unprepared to me. Identify the route and visualise yourself parking at the end of it. That's all? I wasn't sure if I would be comfortable with that. Was that really all there was to it? I decided to reflect on this and, as the session closed, I confirmed I would try to use my psychiatrist's strategy when I started driving again.

After the first couple of art classes, where I felt my drawings were deliberate and confined, I'd decided to use paints and let the brush determine where it went. Almost as if I wasn't in control. I knew I didn't want to colour anything in. I didn't want to be constrained by lines. I felt as if I had been constrained enough and now, I wanted to be free.

Free of pressure. Free from worry. Free of fear. Just free. And I wanted my time in the art class to reflect this.

In one session I used blue, red and green paint and let the brush make random smudges across the page. In another piece I used orange, green, brown, yellow, blue, pink and red paint and allowed the brush to make dots of varying sizes, wherever it wanted. In a later session I drew a small, brown head with a black eye in the bottom left corner. Then with red, blue, orange and green paint I flicked the brush, so it looked like spikes on a hedgehog. Another page showed a sea anemone floating in a rockpool. Using blue and green, I painted its wispy tendrils.

In my final art class, I knew I wanted to continue my thoughts of freedom. I think it signified what I was gaining through the support of the clinic. I picked red, green and blue paint then took the brush with red paint on it. Placing it in the centre of the paper in portrait form, I flicked my wrist. The paintbrush spun out in an arc, leaving a long red streak towards the top right corner. I turned the paper slightly, did the same again with blue paint and another stroke was added. I continued to turn, pick colour and streak, from the same spot, and the brush spiralled away from my wrist, building a vivid picture. As I finished, I was thrilled with what I had created. I'd never be an artist, but I liked the colour variations, the length and contrasting shortness of some of the streaks. The randomness of the shape that had appeared. All from that one central spot. That evening my husband pronounced it his favourite piece and suggested I should put it in a frame and hang it.

I'd had numerous different drivers pick me up either at home or at the clinic, and I'd become used to getting into a range of vehicles and greeting the driver. Interestingly, none of them asked about my illness or what was wrong with me. Towards the end of my attendance at group activities, a big ambulance with two crew, a stretcher and lots of medical paraphernalia arrived. I hadn't been in a vehicle like this before.

One crew member greeted me, opened the door and then pulled out a step, offering me his arm. I thanked him, said I was fine to climb in on my own and made my way to the seat he indicated. Feeling for the seatbelt, I clipped myself in, ready for the off, just as he approached to help buckle me up. The crew member looked surprised to see me in position, seatbelt fastened. I said I was ready to go when they were.

It struck me as we looked at each other that he was obviously used to patients needing help, whereas I was more independent. As I sat thinking about regaining my independence, the crew member took a nearby seat, checked that was OK with me and buckled up. The driver made sure our seatbelts were on and then gently pulled away.

We were going to collect another patient at a hospital across town, I was told. Fine with me. As I walked everywhere, it made a change to look out at different streets, shops and houses from a vehicle. Soon we were drawing up to the entrance and the driver went in to find his patient. The crew member queried if it was OK to ask what had happened to me. Besides my family, neighbours and manager, I'd discussed it mainly with those involved in my care. Surprisingly, I felt happy to tell him about my breakdown. About not being able to look after myself and about attending classes at the clinic. I told him how they gave structure to my day and that I was also receiving psychiatric support.

After being so confused about what had happened, not understanding what was going on, feeling condemned to a life that wasn't mine, I felt happy I could tell someone about my experience so freely. It seemed I could look back on it from a little distance. That signified how far I had come. I listened, while the green overall-clad man told me I looked well and was obviously recovering, watching the driver return with an older lady. After pulling out the step, they helped her into a seat and fastened her seatbelt before we drove off.

My care co-ordinator had said we would develop a plan and complete a traffic light pack.[3] I knew it would involve red, amber and green, and she'd told me it was about recognising signs (not traffic signs, I hoped), but I didn't really understand what she had meant. We met in late January and she explained we would look for clues that showed I was well (green). Things that kept me well and potential triggers that might make me start to feel unwell would also be green. Amber would highlight the first hints of becoming unwell and would be accompanied by an action plan of things to do to help me feel better. Warnings of being unwell would be denoted by red, and we would draft a plan with appropriate action to take if that occurred.

We talked through personal characteristics that showed I was well. We'd covered some of these, such as laughing, being happy in my own company, and being quietly confident and robust when needed, in our initial meeting. Things or situations that had the potential to make me start to feel unwell included direct and indirect criticism of me by others.

Asked to identify helpful activities and ways of managing daily life stresses or potential triggers gave me the opportunity to consider life before I'd become unwell. I also thought about things I had begun to do more recently. As we identified activities such as looking at nature, walks in the country and listening to music, I realised how much fun I was having. My care co-ordinator took notes as we also considered work-related activities, such as having regular de-brief sessions with my manager.

It was hard to think about signs that had indicated I was becoming unwell. It was confronting. I remembered I put off or found it hard to do simple tasks, such as making a shopping list. I had a headache and felt overwhelmed by information. I didn't understand things I was told. The gasman could have been speaking in a foreign language when he advised me about necessary work after our annual check. I forgot I had done things like locking the door or turning down the heating, which meant I had to check and re-check everything. There were so many signs I was becoming unwell. How had I missed them?

As my care co-ordinator continued to write, I remembered a completely unbidden thought I had had a few months before I became ill. It was so surprising, so unexpected, I could still picture myself as it happened. My husband was driving us north through a hilly tree-lined area of road and I was listening as he talked. Suddenly I thought, *I just want to be looked after.* As soon as the words came into my head, I wondered why I'd thought them. What did it mean? Where did the words come from? Why did I want to be looked after? I explained this to my care co-ordinator, who remarked that subconsciously I had perhaps realised that all wasn't well. I just hadn't been able to recognise the signs.

We moved on to plan action I might take if I started to feel unwell again. Top of my list was talking to someone. I knew I hadn't sought help early enough, that I could have talked to my husband, family or manager about my work concerns. I had continued to think I could cope with anything that was thrown at me. I recognised I didn't seek help easily, so it was important to highlight the support I now had, and could turn to, or be referred to, in future: my general practitioner, counsellor, psychiatrist and the mental health clinic. I also recognised activities that provided a distraction for me—baking and handicrafts—where I used my hands. Going for walks, enjoying nature, paying attention to my surroundings, getting exercise and generally looking after myself were other things I thought of for my amber action plan.

As she drew our appointment to a close, my care co-ordinator explained we would focus on red warnings of being unwell in our next meeting. She encouraged me to discuss the plan with my husband; together we might recognise other signs of my wellness (or otherwise). As I left, I thought about how much had happened within the last two months, how much I was learning. I understood I had missed the warning signs of my impending implosion and, although it was uncomfortable reliving these experiences, it seemed important to reflect on and record them fully. They might help me in future.

That night my husband and I discussed the traffic light plan. I was keen to find out if there were other things he had noticed, which we could add. I wanted to make sure I covered every base, because this plan would help keep me well. My husband reminded me that, in the months leading up to my illness, he'd commented I didn't laugh the way I used to. As he said this, I remembered him saying, 'You used to laugh at things', but I hadn't known how to respond. He explained I had a real 'belly laugh', full of gusto and fun, quite loud and a bit infectious. He'd missed my laugh. Also, I hadn't reacted when he tickled me. He used to love tickling me, especially my feet. I would shriek, twist, laugh and squirm to get away when he approached stealthily. But then there was nothing. No reaction. No response to his approach or touch—almost as if I were immune to feeling. I jotted these things down to tell my care co-ordinator.

When I asked him about potential triggers, my husband suggested the threat of redundancy or having to make people redundant. The restructure of the service might mean redundancies. I couldn't bear to think about staff members losing jobs, especially when I knew how difficult things were for them personally and for the service itself.

We also discussed losing someone close to us. Both my 'aunt' and my older uncle had died within two short years of each other, my uncle about eighteen months before my illness. As we spoke, I realised I hadn't dealt with their loss, with what they meant to me. Hadn't talked about them, hadn't looked at pictures, had buried my feelings. I remembered them, of course, but everything was buttoned up inside me. My 'aunt' had featured heavily in my childhood, not only when I had stayed with her, but because of her visits. She would tell us about the family, the animals and all the things that needed to be done on the farm.

When my uncle died, something inside told me laughter had died too. I remembered him taking me as a toddler to the nearest dung heap to dig up worms for fishing. Me with my seaside bucket and spade, digging through the muck, him lying on the bank smoking a cigarette, watching as I did all the work. He declared me too little to go fishing with him, so I never knew if my stinking loot did the trick.

Although he'd been a bit of a devil (lots of drinking and fighting, according to Mum, just because he had to), he matured into a loving and proud husband and father. But it was memories of Hogmanay parties that resonated most when I thought of my uncle. He would arrive with his 'bag'—in the early 1980s, a plastic one filled with cans of Tennent's beer, each featuring a female model. As the years passed, the 'bag' became a sports bag filled with beer, rum, gin, whisky, brandy and my aunt's favourite, peach schnapps. You name it, he had it. As the evening wore on, he became less discerning about his drink. You could guarantee any out-of-date beer would still suit his palate.

My uncle was diagnosed with cancer and died after only a few short months, on Christmas Eve, aged 57. His funeral was held on 31 December. Fitting as one cousin said, because 'he was Mr Hogmanay'. Memories of him swirled around me as I tried to be composed at the service. My sister held me tight. My uncle and his humour, funny walks, his habit of saying 'how?' instead of 'why?' and his striding to stand in front of the fire whenever he visited, irrespective of season, had been a mainstay in my life.

Leaving the church to go to the cemetery, Mum opted to travel with some relatives who weren't familiar with the area. Gran went in the funeral car with my aunt and cousins. Dad, my sister and I followed with other relatives, including my younger uncle and other cousins. Although we knew the town, we hadn't realised there was a one-way traffic system in operation and were held up. We arrived at the cemetery, parked and walked in, amongst old gravestones that had stood the test of time. Something didn't feel right. We reached a gap in the tall stone wall, where the road became a crossroads. As we looked, the cemetery unfolded in front of us. Gravestone upon gravestone to the left and right, continuing for what seemed like miles.

High up on the hill to our left, figures and cars were silhouetted against the sky. We started up the steep hill, trying to go as fast as we could. My cousin puffed as he said they could not proceed without us, reassuring us the three pallbearers in our group were needed. Just before the steepest incline of the hill, we saw people move and the hearse drive away. We'd missed it. I stopped, staring at the dispersing crowd. My uncle had been buried and we weren't there. How had we missed it? Why didn't they wait? I continued up the hill, fury and hurt propelling me forward. I saw Mum as she darted round some relatives saying, 'Oh no, here's Ali . . . I can't face her'. I was desolate. Inconsolable. I hadn't been able to say a final goodbye to my uncle. I walked against the tide of relatives and friends until I reached the graveside. To say a private farewell. My cousin, still puffing, put his arm round me. He told me our uncle would be laughing loudly at us for having missed his burial. To this day, I hope he's right.

I had noted in my traffic light plan that I enjoyed handicrafts and, on one visit, my neighbour invited me to an afternoon beading party that she was hosting. My neighbour's husband said he would be making himself scarce! I hadn't beaded before. I didn't know how to, but my neighbour said she would help me. I looked at some necklaces she had been working on and thought how pretty and professional they looked.

A few afternoons later I sat at her table, while other women arrived with bags and workboxes. They spread their boxes of beads and accoutrements while my neighbour's husband made tea and coffee before heading out. My neighbour threaded a needle and had me choose some beads. Then she showed me how to thread and sew them into a rope, four beads wide. I took over, trying to follow her instructions, but I was distracted by one of the women opposite. She had what I can only describe as a contraption on her head. It was metal. It had what looked like a pair of binoculars sticking out at an angle. While I continued to sew (trying not to prick my finger) she moved the binocular part down. Looking through it she picked up her work, the lenses magnifying the beads below, helping her to see more easily. We sat beading and I listened to the conversation around me—about bead shops with sales, a forthcoming craft afternoon, the health of one of their friends. Usual conversation. All the time I was fascinated by the woman with the headgear. When she turned to look at whoever was speaking, only the lower part of her face could be seen. Above were large round lenses. I had a fun afternoon and although I didn't produce a necklace, I was pleased that I had learned something new.

Over three or four meetings I built my traffic light plan with my care co-ordinator. She encouraged me to continue identifying signals that had shown I was becoming unwell. I remembered a strange mannerism, which occurred a few times when I was driving. Out of nowhere, I had begun to randomly click my tongue. I wasn't aware I was going to do it. It just happened. I didn't understand why I was doing it. Maybe this strange tic was connected. I recognised I had begun to take chances when driving, pulling on to roundabouts when it was safer to wait. This had earned me a few blasts of the horn from concerned drivers. I had also become fixated about parking the car straight. It became usual for me to hop out, assess, jump back in and repark. Another thing I remembered was developing an inability to look people in the eye when I spoke to them. I had started to look slightly to their left or right. Curious. I'd always maintained good eye contact in conversations before.

One session was particularly challenging because it took me back to that night in the river. My care co-ordinator and I agreed it was important to recognise all the signs of becoming unwell. To acknowledge them. To document them, however uncomfortable. I remembered so clearly the thoughts smashing into my head. Hard. Fast. Painful. I hardly had time to deal with one before another slammed into me. How I wanted to get away from them. I didn't know where. I just wanted the thoughts to stop pounding me.

The signs leading up to that night were also painful to deal with. Remembering waking up in the middle of the night. Wandering from room to room. Staring out the window. Trying to open my laptop. How I couldn't be alone, how I followed my husband round the house, how I needed his constant reassurance. And the signs of illness that became apparent over the following weeks—being unable to make decisions, being influenced by others, not trusting my instincts, being directed to do things because I couldn't determine them myself. It was hard to remember how alone and scared I had felt. How I thought I'd never get better. How catastrophically I had thought. As we spoke, my care co-ordinator reminded me of the progress I was making. Reminded me I could look back and see a difference in me then and me now.

We detailed an action plan about what to do if I felt I was becoming unwell again. Challenging my thoughts and making a thought record. Trying to relax and not fighting! Being guided and helped by others, including my general practitioner and, if an urgent referral was necessary, the duty officer. Accident and Emergency was an option if urgent treatment was needed and my care co-ordinator also highlighted the Samaritans and Mental Health helplines. As we ended the session, she explained the clerical staff would type up what we'd prepared so far. In another session we would look at a mental health first aid kit to help keep me well. Also, some advanced treatment directives, so my husband, family and general practitioner were fully aware of the treatment I was happy to receive.

Creative writing was my last class at the clinic. As I waited for my transport, I wondered who might pick me up. The small red car was familiar, and I recognised the elderly male driver. On the way, I told him this was my last session as an acute patient. I would return to the clinic for appointments and to participate in a course. I wanted to thank him, to let him know how much he and the other drivers had helped me. He said how well I was doing and asked if I would do something for him. I said I would, if I could. He asked me to stay beautiful. It was the driver who told me on an earlier pick-up that they liked to share out the beautiful ones. His words really touched me.

I was beginning to think about driving again and discussed this with my husband. He suggested we try it in a staged way. He could join me for short drives, be there if I felt anxious or unsure; we could then go for longer drives. The best laid plans . . . and all that. One day he called to say he'd had car trouble on the way to work. His car had been towed to a garage in a nearby town and he planned to get the train home.

As we drove to pick it up, bowling through country lanes in my small car, I suddenly realised I would have to drive home myself. Strangely, I didn't feel anxious about it; I didn't start to feel tense. Didn't think about which route to take home. I remembered my psychiatrist encouraging me to focus on the endpoint; everything else would just happen. Soon we drew up to the garage and my husband went in to make payment while I moved over to the driving seat. I would follow him home. I changed the seat position, made sure the rear-view mirror gave me a good view and checked my wing mirrors. So far, so good. I felt comfortable in the driving seat. I pictured myself turning into our carport at the end of the journey, took a deep breath and relaxed.

My husband drew his car out the garage and, indicating left, turned into the road. I started the engine, checked my mirrors and indicated to follow. The steering wheel felt good beneath my hands. I had remembered the correct indicator side, and I was driving again. I followed my husband up a hill, the road unknown, marvelling that I was doing this. I was really driving! And I didn't feel tense. I didn't feel worried. It was fun. I was enjoying it. Reaching over, I switched on the radio, something I hadn't done for years because I had needed to concentrate fully to make sure I didn't cause an accident. My previous journeys had been in silence, brow furrowed and window open to keep me cool. In contrast, I was listening to music and smiling, and the temperature felt exactly right.

I saw my husband indicate and pull over to a stop. I followed him and, putting on the handbrake, opened my window when I saw him coming towards me. He leaned in, gave me a big kiss and told me he had no idea where we were! It didn't matter. I was feeling proud. I felt in control and relaxed at the same time. It was a happy drive, the light fading as we reached home, me following my husband into the carport. We hugged and he said how well I'd done. How proud he was. I had driven without the staged plan. I had pictured myself at home and everything had worked out. I felt almost drunk with happiness. Driving that night had been nothing like my previous experiences. I looked forward to doing it again.

Still feeling happy about my driving success, I received a letter inviting me to a meeting with my manager. It was to be held under formal Attendance Management procedures. I had the right to be accompanied by a trade union representative or work colleague. I was not entitled to be accompanied by a friend or family member, although I could request consideration of this, if I asked well in advance of the meeting. I knew such letters had to be written in a precise style, but I found the words and tone frightening, even though that wasn't the intention. I remembered my employment specialist offering to accompany me to meetings with my employer. Having made sure of her availability, I contacted my manager to request permission for her attendance, which was granted. My employment specialist suggested we meet at the clinic and chat about the meeting, as she drove us to my employer's headquarters. It sounded like a good plan; I was nervous and welcomed her support.

My manager and a personnel officer met us both and introductions were made. When my manager and I met in early January, I had only been taking the medication prescribed by the psychiatrist for a short time. Now I could give an update on my progress: I noticed a difference in my mood, which my husband also recognised. I still had some issues with memory and concentration and some difficulty following verbal instructions, but I was working to improve this. My manager commented he also recognised an improvement in me. I said my psychiatrist was pleased with my progress but thought I was still a few months away from returning to work. We discussed ways to overcome the issues I had experienced, including isolation, and I was told I would be based in my employer's headquarters on my return.

My manager informed me of a proposal to move the registration service to another directorate, as part of a wider review of services. If this was approved, I would have a new line manager. We would meet again after my next Occupational Health appointment. Although the aim was to assist me with a sustained return to work, if I couldn't return within the time specified in the formal absence management procedures, other options would be discussed. These included medical redeployment. My manager reminded me of my employer's counselling services, and I explained I had agreed on a plan with the counsellor. We would resume sessions when I was discharged from the clinic and returned to work.

It was invaluable to debrief with my employment specialist on the way back to the clinic. Although the meeting had been pleasant and helpful, I found its formal nature challenging. I was worried I might have to consider options if I couldn't return to work within the specified period. My employment specialist suggested I continue to focus on my recovery, be guided by my psychiatrist on an appropriate return date and remember the procedure was there to help. We agreed to meet again when we received the formal record of the meeting, to cover any other questions or concerns I had. That night, snug in my husband's arms, I told him about the meeting—how my progress had been recognised, but how I feared not being well enough in time to resume work. He held me tightly and reiterated my employment specialist's words, that I should focus on getting better. Positive thinking. With that, he began to sing,

CHAPTER 7

March–May 2011 – Recovery

The anxiety management course at the clinic began in March. Through appointments with my psychiatrist and therapist, I had recognised that my need for perfection and avoidance of situations had contributed to the pressure I felt at work. Without exercise, close friends or hobbies, I had left myself vulnerable. Although I had never thought of myself as someone who was particularly anxious, I was keen to find out more about managing anxiety.

Reading my book in the waiting room, I tried to guess which of my fellow occupants might attend the course. I didn't recognise anyone. As the big hand reached the hour on the clock, my care co-ordinator announced the anxiety management course. Eight or so of us walked through to one of the group rooms, which had chairs in a circle with a handout on each.[4]

My care co-ordinator and her male colleague introduced themselves as our facilitators. The course would last six weeks, with each session one and a half hours in duration. The availability of the safe room was mentioned, in case anyone felt the need to have time to themself. We each then made brief introductions, explaining what we hoped to get out of the course, before going to make tea or coffee in the kitchen. We moved around the small space with the politeness of people who hadn't met before, showing one another where the cups were and passing the milk around. As we made our way back to the room, I chatted briefly to a man who looked a bit older than me, before noticing a late participant, the other creative writer from my Thursday class. We acknowledged each other by eye contact before the course began.

We started discussing what anxiety was. We all knew the effects of it and, looking round the room, it was obvious it could affect people of any age, race or background. Our facilitator reminded us of some symptoms: feeling faint or dizzy, heart pounding, excess sweating, a 'lump' in the throat, et cetera. We all nodded knowingly. As we shared symptoms, including my feeling of being constantly 'charged', it became apparent how wide-ranging, unpleasant and scary they could be.

Our course handout explained anxiety could affect not only the body, but also thoughts and potentially lifestyles. When we were anxious, our posture could change. We might stoop or hunch over. Clench our fists. Furrow our brows. As we talked, I remembered my usual comfortable seated position changing to one where I was perched on the edge of the seat, where my legs were not crossed but entwined like a vine. Where every muscle felt taut. We learned anxiety could make us think we couldn't do something or, if we tried, something bad would happen. We would feel ill or embarrass ourselves. And because we didn't like the uncomfortable feelings of anxiety, it could seem easier to avoid situations and decide we were too frightened to go outside or alone—stopping us from doing things we might really want to do.

The facilitator reminded us that everyone felt some anxiety and that was good! It was helpful to be alert when crossing the road. Anxiety put us on guard. It was positive when attending an interview or giving a performance. Anxiety spurred us on. But, if our anxiety levels got too extreme, or lasted too long, then there could be serious consequences. For me, being reminded anxiety wasn't all bad was almost a revelation! I'd spent so many months wanting to slay the anxiety dragon. Beat it senseless. Rid it from my life until I was completely relaxed. I'd forgotten a certain amount of anxiety was a good thing.

We were reminded the body has a 'fight or flight' response. Primitive man, faced with danger, would either fight or run away fast. His feelings of anxiety would reduce. We weren't fighting wild animals, though. We didn't necessarily realise when tension was maintained in our bodies. One useful way to diffuse it was regular exercise.

Even though I'm married to an anatomist, even though I've heard more than the average lay-person about muscles, nerves, tissues, fascia, tendons, cartilage and bones, I hadn't heard about the autonomic nervous system. We found out it determines how anxious or relaxed we are. It has two branches, one to prepare us for immediate danger—think increased breathing and release of adrenaline. The other is to relax us, to turn off our fight or flight response. The facilitator explained if we got too keyed up, too anxious and didn't relax or exercise to release our tension, we could feel distress.

She asked us to imagine a situation where we felt highly stressed. If we continued to stay in the situation, what would happen? Would our anxiety worsen? Stay the same? Or would it lessen? We all made suggestions, before she confirmed experiments had shown anxiety lessens as a person becomes more used to a situation. I thought back to times when I've spoken in public. I found them nerve-racking but enjoyable—maybe I wasn't not the only one? My left knee would shake noticeably when I started to speak. I had no way to control it. It had a mind of its own. Gradually, though, it would begin to shake a little less, then calm down, allowing me to focus on my words and the audience around me. So, this seemed to make sense. The facilitator explained if we left a stressful situation, it could be harder to face it in future. We might start to avoid it all together. Also, we wouldn't become familiar with the situation and recognise we were becoming less anxious.

'Faulty thinking' was then introduced—negative and irrational thoughts we possibly all have. You might know the type. 'I'm so stupid, why do I always get things wrong?' you say after making a simple mistake. Although I hadn't considered it before, the facilitator explained these types of negative thoughts could affect our anxiety level, make us feel worse. She said we often expected too much of ourselves and were disappointed again and again.

By this stage, I was recognising some things about myself. Although I liked to think I was a 'glass-half-full' type of person, the reality was I could be quite negative and hard on myself. After I gave a talk where I thought I might have said something inappropriate, I stopped speaking in public (even declining to give a farewell speech when I moved jobs). I went over and over what I had said, wishing I could turn back the clock. Replaying it. Thinking about what others must have thought. Feeling embarrassed. Berating myself. Instead of reflecting on what I could have done differently, like planning the talk rather than speaking off the cuff, I decided, wherever possible, not to put myself in a position where I had to speak in public again; I avoided it.

The facilitator explained the course would help us recognise anxiety as normal. It would teach us ways to control our anxiety and would inform us how to keep it at moderate levels, rather than the extreme levels we had experienced. We would learn how to relax, how to challenge our faulty or negative thinking, and discover techniques to help us problem-solve and improve our social skills.

The course would be challenging, we were warned—not that the facilitators wanted to put us off. They wanted us to be aware we would reach into ourselves and relive experiences, which we'd be asked to share if we felt able. They also stressed we needed to assess ourselves whether we were ready for the course. Although the larger clinical team had agreed with our inclusion and thought it would help us, if we ourselves didn't feel ready, then it was probably better not to proceed. The facilitator reassured us, in gentle tones, the decisions we made would be respected. There would be future courses to join. One final thing: the course was a self-help one. We needed to be prepared to put in the work over six weeks and attend regularly if we were to get the most from the experience. Completing the course would demonstrate to us that we had achieved it through our own endeavours.

The facilitators then introduced the contrast muscle relaxation. They explained it would help us become aware of what tension felt like around our body and how nice it felt when that tension was relaxed. We sat, eyes closed, as the facilitator asked us to move around our body, clenching and releasing muscle groups. We began with hands, clenching fists and feeling the tension in our knuckles and up our arms. After holding for a slow count of three, we released our fists and were asked to notice the warmth and looseness in our hands and forearms. The contrast between the taut, tight fists and the loose, open hands was marked. Before moving on to upper arms, the facilitator checked that we understood and recognised the relaxed state. We pressed elbows into sides, counted for three and released. Again, I felt the warm looseness of relaxation. We raised eyebrows and crinkled foreheads, before releasing. We screwed up eyes, wrinkled noses and clenched jaws, before letting go. Chins were pressed into chests, heads tilted forward and then relaxed. Lower backs were arched and shoulder blades pulled close to each other, then loosened. Stomachs were pulled in, almost so tummy buttons hit spines, before releasing. Finally, legs were straightened and feet pulled up so toes pointed to faces, before slackening. Even though I'd tried to relax with the CD the Crisis Team had given me, this was the first time I truly felt the difference between tension and relaxation. It was lovely.

The facilitators gave us assignments to prepare for the next session: a stress diary and a relaxation breathing practise to be completed each day. We were told to breathe in through our noses for a slow count, hold for a count of one, then breathe out for longer than we breathed in. As we practised, the count would become longer. It was important that the exhale breath remained longer than the inhale to help us relax. We were also to practise the contrast muscle relaxation and identify personal tension spots—places in our body which we knew, or discovered, were particularly tense.

As we traipsed out the room, saying goodbye to the facilitators, I realised how much we'd covered. I had learned things and heard about others' experiences. I had spent so many months feeling frightened. Alone. Not understanding what was happening or why. Now I knew I was going to find out, share my experiences and listen to others. All of this would help determine ways to make sure this didn't happen to me again.

The next day I drove to the clinic to meet my employment specialist. My employer had sent a letter with notes from our recent meeting, which I'd read. Now we were going to review it together, so she could answer any queries or offer reassurance. As I entered the car park, I thought about being driven and dropped off there by the ambulance and volunteer drivers. Even though I was thrilled to be driving on my own and, even more, surprised I was enjoying it, I missed those little interactions—the sharing of news, the eating of sweets, the laughter at the stories they told.

Although the meeting with my manager had been positive, I had found it unnerving to read a written summary of it. I had tried to focus on the positives—they thought I looked well, my consultant was happy with my progress and I would be moving to a new office location on my return—but it was hard to ignore what I perceived as negatives. My employment specialist again reassured me. We were all working together to return me to my role, healthy, happy and confident. If my psychiatrist thought I needed more time before returning, then I should follow his advice. I shouldn't feel under pressure to return before I was ready. The discussion about other options, such as medical redeployment, wasn't meant to frighten or punish me. It was simply to make me aware of what was available under the formal procedure. I knew she was right, but the fear I had felt reading the letter alone for the first time highlighted to me how fragile I still was, how vulnerable people in this situation were. I'd never really thought about it before. As I left the clinic, I reflected on how much more I was learning from this experience.

I thought my husband and I had done some good work on my traffic light plan. At our next meeting, my care co-ordinator prompted me with gentle questions and probed some of the feelings I relayed to her. She checked with me as she took notes to make sure she captured the essence of what I told her. She elicited my views on treatment if I became unwell again, noting I might fear becoming dependent on medication; that I welcomed the support of the Crisis Team, psychiatrist and therapist; and I might need to attend day services to help provide structure if I couldn't manage this myself. When she asked me about unacceptable treatment, I didn't really have any idea. I remembered Mum had chosen to look after me at home, rather than going to hospital, so we agreed hospitalisation would be a last resort. We listed the people involved in my care, who I could call on again. We detailed how they could help me: listening to my thoughts, worries and concerns; providing suggestions and drafting an action plan to help me get better; and reviewing my medication or deciding if further medication was necessary.

My care co-ordinator asked how I would help myself get better if I was in the same situation again. I reflected on what had made a difference to me: writing a 'mantra' to remind me of the people who told me I would get better, so I could read and re-read it to help me believe in my ability to get well; writing a small list of basic tasks each day and scoring them off when done, so I could feel a sense of achievement; starting with little goals and discussing my progress with family; doing things I enjoyed, rather than things I felt I ought to do; asking for help; taking medication as prescribed and 'being a pupil'— doing what I was told and learning how to get better.

Together we discussed a mental health first aid kit, which would contain things to give me a lift if I felt unwell. Items of significance were recommended, and suggestions included a photo of family, friend or pet; a CD of favourite music; a candle; a magazine; some chocolate; something collected; a game; a book; something creative to do; a sketchbook or notebook; and pens. I mulled over what I would include in my own kit while my care co-ordinator explained the traffic light plan would be shared with my general practitioner. She would also give me cards with the details typed on, so I could carry them in my wallet. I felt as if everything had been thought of. It had been such a useful exercise, enabling me to think, reflect and talk about becoming unwell—recognising the signs I had overlooked and being positive about how I would go forward in future. My care co-ordinator explained, as the session concluded, there was no reason to think I would have another breakdown. I was learning what had led to it and was working on strategies to keep me well. The anxiety management course was an important part of that. However, if I recognised one or two signs of becoming unwell again, I shouldn't worry but use my traffic light plan to get things back on track.

My employment specialist was driving us to my employer's headquarters for another meeting, telling me more about her role and what it entailed. Since the last meeting, my psychiatrist had provided a report to my employer's Occupational Health doctor, confirming my diagnosis and advising I was not yet fit to return to work. He suggested a return in June. In the meeting I explained I was continuing to improve but remained on the same levels of medication and would be guided on a return date by the psychiatrist. Although I had thought only about the negative aspects of returning to work, I explained I was now feeling more positive.

My manager confirmed the service would be transferred to a new directorate and, subject to the approval of my psychiatrist, he would arrange a workplace visit to meet my new line manager. We could discuss the changes that had occurred over the last few months, developments and plans, and my individual needs for a return to work. We reviewed the dates of my psychiatrist and Occupational Health appointments, so my manager could begin to plan the workplace visit. He was keen to emphasise it would be postponed if my psychiatrist advised this.

We considered the arrangements for my accrued annual leave and formally extended the timeframe of the Absence Management Procedure, to take account of my expected return to work on a phased basis. I was concerned about receiving payment when I wasn't returning to full-time work because we were taxpayer-funded. After all my worries about surviving financially, bargain-hunting and eating leftovers, this seemed another indicator of my return to well-being. I was thinking of other people. I wasn't focused only on myself.

The personnel officer confirmed I couldn't refuse payment, explaining this was a 'protected period' to reintegrate me back to the workplace. I couldn't be treated differently to anyone else in the same situation. I felt content I had at least raised the possibility of not receiving payment. We agreed our next meeting would focus on the details of my phased return and arrangements for it. I left feeling happy with the agreed outline plan and more confident about returning to work.

Later that same afternoon, the second session of the anxiety management course was held. The man I'd greeted in the kitchen the previous week wasn't in the waiting room and, when our class assembled, it was obvious several others weren't there either. The facilitators explained the man I remembered had been offered a job and so wouldn't be able to continue the course. Those of us there quietly offered our congratulations. Even though I'd been with my manager that morning, even though we were planning my return to work, it seemed far away. But it was nice to hear someone from our group was now well enough to work. Some other participants had decided the course wasn't for them at this stage.

The facilitators encouraged us to share our experiences during the session, especially given the smaller numbers, as we looked at physical tension control. We began by discussing the self-help assignments from the previous session. Asked to list any tension spots we observed during relaxation, I commented I had noted tension in my neck and jaw. I had suffered from painful temporomandibular joint problems in my late twenties, so this wasn't a surprise.

The facilitators reviewed what we'd learned about the fight or flight response, reminding us it was a natural mechanism designed to protect ourselves. If we became excessively anxious, they explained, the physical signs could be very unpleasant. They asked us to name some of the signs that we recognised in ourselves, and the pounding heart was top of the list!

I recounted being in bed, unable to sleep while at Mum and Dad's, my heart beating so loud and fast I was sure it was going to jump out my chest. The faster it went, the more worried I became something nasty would happen. Despite trying to distract myself, all I could hear was my heart thudding. I was so frightened—didn't know what to do. Finally, I had taken diazepam. I had hated those tablets, resisted taking them. It was a sign of how alarmed I had been. The facilitators reiterated when we were anxious, the heart beats stronger and faster to carry blood to and from our muscles. The oxygen in the blood sets us up ready to take flight or fight back. If we didn't use up this extra energy through exercising, it could feel distressing. From my experience that night, I agreed wholeheartedly.

Feeling breathless was another sign of anxiety; our lungs worked harder to get more oxygen into our bloodstream. In dangerous situations, this would help us think more clearly about what to do to protect ourselves. From the nods around the room, it was clear breathlessness was also a familiar symptom. The facilitators explained that, again, exercise helpfully burned off extra oxygen. If we didn't exercise, the gases in our blood might become unbalanced, leading to feelings of dizziness.

The next response was tense or shaky muscles. When we feel anxious, we automatically tense our muscles. I listened while others shared their experiences of shakiness before admitting to the horrible buzzing I had felt in my legs—the unrelenting feeling of being 'charged'. For me, it was the most frightening sign of all. We were told shakiness was linked to the release of the hormone adrenaline into our bloodstream. This was to enable us to react appropriately to danger. Move quickly. Keep us going until we were away from danger. If we remained still, the adrenaline could have a negative effect, making us feel weak.

It was helpful to understand why my body had reacted the way it did. As a group, we continued to discuss the different responses anxiety produced, including nausea and digestive problems. Under stress our digestive system shuts down to divert energy to muscles, priming them for action. This can lead to 'butterflies', diarrhoea, needing to urinate often or having a dry mouth. Increased sweating was another response. The blood flows to surface muscles, so we might feel hot, sweaty and flushed. We might experience visual disturbances. Under stress our eyesight seems clearer to help spot signs of danger. When this wears off, our vision may become blurry. If anxiety isn't relieved by exercise or relaxation, the demands placed on our bodies to maintain the fight or flight state can make us tired or lethargic and can lead to difficulty sleeping.

We also learned some people have a different response to fight or flight. Instead, they become pale and cold. They might faint if their blood pressure drops significantly. This is a 'faint–freeze' response, which can also be seen in the animal kingdom where some pretend to be dead rather than fight or flee.

The facilitators explained the autonomic nervous system is an involuntary system. We can't tell it what to do, like moving hands or feet. Of the two branches, the sympathetic is the arousal system, which readies us for fight or flight. The parasympathetic branch is responsible for helping us sleep, digest food and rest. The good news, we were told, was that only one of these branches could work at any one time. Although a reminder of what we had learned in the previous session, the significance of this information wasn't lost on me.

Even though I couldn't tell my body to stop being anxious, I could learn how to relax.

Being relaxed meant keeping awful anxiety symptoms at bay, as the mind influenced the body. I could help myself. That was important. I didn't want to rely on others. I didn't want to have to be looked after, compensated in some way as if I had a deficit. I wanted to be 'capable me' again. If I could help myself achieve this, so much the better. I was determined to learn relaxation skills so my muscles were relaxed, my mind and body calmer.

We talked more about the 'anxiety posture': furrowed brows, leaning forward, hands in fists, arms tight around us, legs crossed. A lot of us had recognised, it transpired, the anxiety posture! Between sessions I had deliberately tried to sit in a more relaxed way. Keeping both feet on the floor, without crossing my legs, seemed a good way to avoid the tension that prevailed when I sat with my legs crossed. Also, I found just being aware of how I was sitting was helpful. I could keep check. If I felt tense, I could use the contrast muscle relaxation technique we'd been taught, to release the tension.

We had muscles that tensed us and other muscles that relaxed us, the facilitators said. Just as our 'arousal' and 'relaxing' systems couldn't both work at the same time, these different muscle groups also had to work independently. So, if we relaxed, then we couldn't be tense. More good news I thought! An exercise based on *Simple Relaxation*[5] made use of the fact that both muscle groups couldn't work simultaneously.

Relaxation was good for us. It should be part of our daily routine, the facilitators told us. That didn't mean we should lie on the sofa watching a movie. That was something nice to do, but it wasn't relaxing.

Did we take any exercise? Since stopping driving, I had walked much more. I told the group this and about how much better I felt, getting fresh air and seeing the world around me. We didn't look like a particularly energetic bunch. We were all different shapes and sizes, but we were reminded exercise would improve our health and increase our energy and stamina. Not only that, it would improve our appearance, help us meet other people and increase our confidence. All told, there were lots of benefits and we would feel better with regular exercise in our lives. We didn't have to be 'sporty'. There was an exercise for everyone. I had really enjoyed the tai chi sessions at the clinic, so I resolved to see if this could be my form of exercise.

To finish, the facilitators led a simple relaxation. They reminded us to choose a regular time to repeat the exercise at home. We should also make sure we were ready and had no little chores to distract us! We chose either to lie down on the floor or remain sitting in an upright chair with a headrest. Another alternative was to sit in a chair with a pillow on top of a table, with our head and upper body resting on it. Before we started, we placed our hands flat on our abdomens beneath the rib cage, to check we were using the lower part of our chest to breathe. We could feel the tension ease as we breathed out. The facilitator quietly told us thoughts would come into our heads. We should just let them go gently, not engage with them. They wanted us to learn to notice our body. Was it tense or relaxed? We would need to concentrate. Unlike the previous relaxation technique, we wouldn't tense our muscles before relaxing them. We would simply move the body part and then stop.

Quietly the facilitator encouraged us to move our shoulders down towards our feet before stopping. Did our neck feel longer? Were our shoulders lowered? We moved our elbows moved away from our sides, then bent the elbows slightly and stopped. Were our upper arms away from our sides? Was there a big angle at our elbows? Then our hands— we stretched fingers and thumbs while keeping wrists supported. Stop. Did our fingers feel stretched out? Were they separated and resting? We turned our hips outwards before stopping. Had our thighs moved outwards? Were our kneecaps facing outwards? We moved our knees slightly until they were comfortable. Did we enjoy the feeling of comfort in our knees? Pushed toes away from faces, bent at the ankle, then stopping. Were our feet dangling and feeling heavy? Next, we pushed our body into the chair or floor. Stop. Were we aware of the weight of our body? Then we pushed our head back into the support before stopping again. Were we aware of the weight of our head? The facilitator encouraged us to focus on breathing, gently inhaling through the nose, noticing the lower ribs fall inwards and downwards as we breathed out. Moving to our heads, we let our lower jaw drop and then stopped. Did we notice the separation between teeth, jaw and lips? We pressed our tongue downwards and stopped. Did we feel the tongue lying loosely in our mouth? We closed our eyes and stopped. Did we feel our eyelids resting gently? Finally, we smoothed our foreheads from eyebrows upwards. Did we feel them relax?

As we ended, the facilitator encouraged us to repeat the exercise or think of some pleasant theme, allowing our thoughts to wander. Otherwise, they suggested we choose a song or poem to think of while we relaxed our body. Thoughts would persist in trying to interrupt our relaxation, but we should simply let them go. We finished by slowly stretching, yawning and opening our eyes before resuming our seats.

Time seemed to have passed very quickly. Again, I thought how much I had learned during the session. I found it helpful to hear the experiences of others. It was reassuring to know I wasn't the only one affected by anxiety. Our homework was to practise simple relaxation and list the early-warning signs that signalled the rise of our anxiety levels. The facilitators stressed this was the first indication of becoming anxious, not a full-blown panic attack. We said our goodbyes before heading back to reception.

What does it feel like to get better? It's difficult to capture the essence of it. I found it happened gradually, without me realising. Waking up in the morning, my first thought was no longer to question whether I was getting better, but to wonder what I would do that day. It doesn't seem appropriate to use words like 'reborn' or phrases like 'moving from winter to spring' to describe the change in my mood and demeanour. Everything became vibrant. Colours weren't just bright, but brilliant. Everything was more—not simply happy, but ecstatic. Not just inclined, but galvanised. What had been dull and quiet was now vivid and loud. And it was incredible.

Later that week I drove to meet a colleague in the town where I had worked. She was one of the two I had seen that last day at work in September. I had wondered if I would be overcome with memories, driving that familiar route and seeing her for the first time since then. Despite this I felt relaxed and curious, rather than tense and nervous. Such a lot had changed since then. Now, because I knew I was getting better, I was happy to meet my colleague and share what had happened. We met in a café and after hugging, she said how hard she found it not to get in touch. The staff had been instructed not to contact me, because I was absent with work-related stress. She commented how well I looked! It was true. I had filled out, losing the gaunt framework that had frightened me before Christmas. I regained my smile and happy disposition. I told her of my experiences—although not my night-time river one—including the staff I had met at the clinic and the support I had received. She asked if she could tell me a few things about work and I was happy to listen. I knew I would be returning. I felt differently about it now. I really enjoyed seeing her and felt happy driving home. I felt I had reached another recovery milestone.

I was still feeling happy, pleased with how well I was doing, a few days later as I crossed the road to the clinic after parking in the car park opposite. I had driven, radio playing, without any concern. I had resisted temptation, not checking to see how straight my parking was. I hadn't reparked, either. Driving was just one thing I was feeling different about. Waiting for the third anxiety management course session, a man said hello to me. I looked at him but didn't recognise him. He asked how art classes were going? Gradually I realised I had met him before Christmas. This was the man whose line drawings of birds I had admired. I remembered him with the greyness I associated with illness. Now he had colour in his face. Sparkling eyes. As I got up to go to the session, I apologised for not recognising him, told him how well he looked. We smiled together, as if we were conspirators in wellness!

I greeted the other participants and noticed there were more of us than at the last session. In what was becoming a pattern, we discussed our progress during the previous week. As I became more used to simple relaxation, I had begun to enjoy it more. But I preferred the contrast muscle relaxation method. We shared our early-warning anxiety signs. Some began to feel hotter, others felt shoulders and neck tensing up. For some, their breathing had become faster. What was apparent was different people had different signs of impending anxiety.

The facilitators explained we would now look at relaxation in action. As we each knew our own personal tension hot-spots and early signs of anxiety, we would develop ways to relax when needed. It might be on a plane, in the supermarket or at a party. After all, we couldn't suddenly say, 'Stop everyone, I'm feeling stressed. Fetch me a bed. Turn off the lights. I need to do a relaxation exercise'. We needed to identify and respond before tension took hold, irrespective of where or when that was. We would use only the amount of tension our body needed for a task. We would observe how much tension we used when sitting, standing, walking and at work/play. Then we would adjust our posture and relax to feel the difference.

We got up to walk around the room, taking care to avoid chairs and other participants. The facilitator encouraged us to soften our muscles as we walked. To put our feet down less forcefully, to feel as if we were walking on marshmallows. Everything was soft. As we walked, I realised I hadn't considered before how much tension there was in my legs. I decided where I was going and then put every effort into getting there as quickly as possible. I tried to make my legs feel lighter as I walked. After sharing observations, we were asked to sit and notice where we held tension. I felt I was pressing into the seat. My hips and lower back were tight. I moved forward a little and consciously tried to make my seated pose less rigid.

Then we stood in various places around the room to assess the tension we used to stand. I knew my lower back could become very tense from travelling on the tube in London. As seats were scarce during rush hour and I'm short, I often stood in the corner by the door, my feet apart and my lower back fixed to help me balance as the tube accelerated and decelerated. I could feel the familiar tautening in my back. Conscious of the instruction to change posture and relax, I tried to move. It was difficult to find a different standing position. I breathed in. Expanded my chest. Started to think about having an imaginary eraser. I pictured myself 'rubbing out' tense muscles in my lower back with a circular motion. It seems strange, but it helped. As we retook our seats and shared our assessment of tension, I remembered cleaning the birdbath some months before. It was a small, stone bath, that lay among the stones on the path. Using a watering can and brush, I scrubbed and scraped. I used as much force as I could to remove dirt and water stains. When finished, I was surprised my head and facial muscles hurt. My shoulders and upper arms were very tight. Maybe this was an example of not thinking about how much tension I used to carry out tasks? I decided to pay more attention and use my imaginary eraser to see if I could make my muscles softer.

After a short break, we moved to exercises to help us relax quickly. First, a breathing control exercise. As one, we all took a slow, deep breath as the facilitator reminded us to use our diaphragm. As we breathed out slowly, we were asked to feel the tension ebbing away. We repeated this three times, before checking our posture and noticing how relaxed we felt.

Then, we learned a mini relaxation exercise that we could use in an emergency. The facilitator told us to stand (although it could be done seated) with feet slightly apart. Breathe in deeply and count to three. As we did this, we were to stretch our arms and hands away from our body. After making sure our shoulders were lowered, we were to bring our arms back to hang loosely by our sides. Exhaling slowly, we counted to three then lifted our head to smile and relax our facial muscles. We practised this a few times before I burst into giggles, as another female participant had nicknamed it the 'panicking penguin' move, due to the arm flapping!

As the session drew to a close, we discussed feeling tense. What made one person tense didn't necessarily affect another. We each responded differently. The facilitators encouraged us to think about what made us particularly anxious. It might be going out alone, taking public transport or attending a social gathering. Whatever it was, we should try to tackle it using the techniques we'd been shown. They wanted us to find out how differently we could feel when we faced difficult things.

Our assignment was to practise the everyday breathing and emergency 'panicking penguin' relaxation methods. We should make a list of thoughts that went through our mind when anxious. We were now halfway through the course, and I thought everyone was generous in their contributions to the discussion. Leaving the clinic, I crossed the road to my little car.

Over a regular afternoon coffee, my neighbour suggested I might like to join her at an afternoon tatting session. We travelled with her friend, who had been so kind and understanding at my first tatting experience. As we drove to the nearby home of a tatting stalwart, they told me about our hostess. She was in her early 90s but still a sprightly, engaged tatter, responsible for organising an upcoming one-day tatting workshop.

When we arrived, the door was opened by a smiling, small lady in a lovely green skirt suit with a beautiful brooch pinned to her lapel. After welcoming us, she showed us to her sitting room, arranged with chairs and tables ready for handicraft activity. As the three of them chatted, I took out my current piece of tatting, a colourful butterfly. Other ladies arrived, only one of whom I'd met before at my neighbour's house. I wasn't sure of the format of the afternoon, but I was happy to listen to the chatter around me while I concentrated on my tatting.

I became aware the conversation had ceased and, when I looked up, our hostess was standing in the middle of the floor with a notebook in her hand. Clearing her throat, she proceeded to call the meeting to order and announced the date and location of the workshop. Asking for volunteers, she listed the tasks she had drawn up to make the day a success. Our hostess took notes, confirming who would do what before moving on to recount news of other tatting activities and showing and sharing a pattern she had found. It seemed to be extremely intricate and way beyond anything I could ever achieve, I was sure! In answer to a question, she confirmed there would be a feature display of tatting at the workshop. We should all submit something, she said.

The formal part of the afternoon over, she disappeared into the kitchen before wheeling out a trolley. Plates of scones and sponge cake, which she had made earlier that day, nestled on top. I spent a lovely time with some interesting people and was incredibly grateful to my neighbour and her friend for including me.

When I was out shopping one day, dressed in my familiar tracksuit bottoms, green zip-up fleece and stripy hat, I remembered I needed to make a doctor's appointment. Walking up the hill past the bank and off-licence, I caught up with a small group who were taking up the whole pavement—a young woman on the inside, a man with tattoos on his neck and a flat-cap in the middle, and a small boy with a tricycle. They ambled along as if they had all the time in the world. I couldn't decide how to get past. Cars were parked by the pavement, so I couldn't nip on to the street to get by. There wasn't enough room between the woman and the shopfronts. Should I ask them to allow me past? While I was debating this internally and hovering behind them, the man suddenly turned and yelled, 'Oh for f&*%s sake, just pass, will you?' I moved between him and the boy and made my way further up the hill before turning back and asking, 'Did you just swear at me?'

Before the man could respond, the woman approached and gripped my left arm tightly. Looking directly into my face, she asked me to leave it, on today of all days, could I please just leave it? I didn't understand. Why was the day important? Something in her eyes, a pleading desperation, made me turn away. Without further comment, I powered up the hill without a backward glance, annoyance at the man's rudeness fuelling my steps.

I made my appointment before turning back down the hill. As I walked, I thought my handling of the situation was a sign I wasn't completely well yet. Ordinarily, I would have challenged someone about behaviour like that. He didn't know what was happening to me. He didn't know the impact his words, and the way he said them, had on me. As I continued, I decided if I saw the group again, I would speak to them. Tell them how upset I felt. Pleased with my decision, as if I was regaining a little bit of myself and my identity, I walked past some shops.

As I crossed the railway bridge, I saw the man, tricycle in one hand, holding on to the small boy with the other. They were approaching the ticket machine as I reached them. The woman was nowhere to be seen. I was determined to say something, but I didn't have time to plan. 'Excuse me', I said. 'I realise you might be having a bad day, but can I just say something?' The man turned to me and said yes. I told him I was recovering from a nervous breakdown. That, sometimes, I found it hard to be decisive. That he might not realise how much his outburst had upset me. Looking at me, he replied, 'I'm going to prison tomorrow, probably for six years, and my girlfriend has just walked away from me'.

I didn't know how to respond. What could I say? I had no idea about his situation. How could I? Just as he didn't know about mine.

I told him I was sorry to hear that, wished him well, and said I would keep him and the little boy in my thoughts. I left them standing by the ticket machine as I walked away.

In late March, my husband told me we would be invited to dinner at the home of a colleague. They were both members of the local medical trust board. He wanted to check if I was happy to go. It would be only the second social occasion I'd attended since the previous September. Thinking back to the students' ball in December, where I had felt completely detached from everyone around me, I felt nervous. We discussed how much I'd improved since then. My husband reassured me he would sit next to me, if I thought that would help. I wanted to go. I wanted to reclaim my life, enjoy things I used to. But I was worried. It might be obvious I'd had a serious mental health issue and I'd let my husband down. Somehow, I would embarrass both of us. My husband gently told me that that wouldn't happen. It was my decision, but he would like me to go with him.

I thought about the forthcoming evening. What would I wear? How would I be? Would I take part in conversation or sit quietly? Would I understand what was going on around me, after so long not understanding? Would I feel part of the gathering or like someone looking in from the outside? Would I drop things—cutlery, food, drinks? Or, would it be fun? Would I get to meet new people? Would it be nice to be somewhere other than our sitting room in the evening? Would there be interesting conversation?

As I thought, I realised I had been meeting new people since I started attending the clinic. The drivers who took me to classes. The staff who helped with my recovery. The others who attended classes with me. All these people treated me with kindness and without judgment. So, I shouldn't build this up into something it wasn't; it was an extension of the life I was living. I was getting better. I needed to start showing I was me again. This was an opportunity to do that.

I decided I would go and that we would take a small gift. I told my husband my decision and that I would make a fruit loaf (one of Mum's recipes). He was pleased and thought a homemade bakery item would be apt. Still slightly nervous but with a plan in place, I began to prepare. I remembered my psychiatrist telling me to visualise the endpoint I wanted to achieve. I pictured myself leaving a house, hand-in-hand with my husband. Clothes clean and fresh, without food spilled on them. Waving to a couple in the doorway. Everything else in between would just happen.

We stood on the doorstep of a house not too far from our own, me clutching my husband's hand tightly with one hand and clasping a fruit loaf in the other. I was shaking. My husband could feel it. But I knew my anxiety would lessen. I had learned this in the first week of the anxiety management course. I didn't feel worried by the shaking; I just waited for it to subside.

Our host welcomed us, showed us inside, and introduced us to his wife and three children. I handed over my homemade gift. He seemed surprised I had made it myself, double-checking with me. My husband continued to hold my hand as we were given drinks and started to talk. We had arrived early, which was nice because I wasn't confronted by having to walk into a room of people. I could feel myself begin to relax. After two other couples arrived, we moved into the dining room. Sitting next to our host, I asked how long he had lived in the house and what his background was, while conversation continued around us. Over a delicious meal I learned about the work four of them did on the trust board, each having something different to contribute. I was able to follow what was being said. Occasionally I added the odd comment from a patient perspective, although I didn't feel the need to explain about my experience. Somewhere in the evening, I noticed I was having fun. My concerns about embarrassing myself, spilling things and not being part of the group went unrealised. I had a super time with lovely people. As we left and I walked up the path hand-in-hand with my husband, waving to our host while his wife checked the children in bed, I told my husband how much I had enjoyed it.

A few days later my husband said his friend had emailed to say the loaf was delicious! Plus, I was lovely, and he wondered how my husband had persuaded me to hitch up with him. It was a funny email that did wonders for my self-confidence and I've kept it to this day.

Once again, our small group was gathered in a circle, cups in hand, as we began our fourth session of the anxiety management course. We reviewed our homework—the 'everyday' and 'emergency' relaxation methods. I found the 'everyday' relaxation, using only the required amount of tension, difficult when walking. I had to concentrate on my posture as I felt tension particularly in my shoulders and arms. I found the seated position much easier to relax in. I tended to clasp my hands tightly together, so I had focused on relaxing my hands and arms. I tensed my shoulders, arms and lower back particularly when standing up straight. I had to concentrate hard on how I was holding my body to release the tension.

When it came to the 'emergency' relaxation, we laughed along with the woman who named the 'panicking penguin' manoeuvre, as she told us about using it in a stressful situation. I hadn't practised it (I hadn't been in a stressful situation) but I had noticed tension markedly leave my body when we'd tried it in the last session. I thought it was a useful tip.

We had been asked to make a list of ideas and thoughts that went through our minds when we were anxious. Just as people experienced different signs of anxiety, there were a variety of thoughts and ideas. I fed back: 'I don't know what to do', 'Am I doing this well enough?', 'I don't know where to go' and 'People will look at me and see that I don't know what to do or where to go'. As we shared, the facilitators commented there were lots of individual beliefs in the room, different ways of thinking and diverse behaviours. They taught us about the ABCs of activating events, beliefs and consequences. Waving at someone who doesn't acknowledge was an example of an activating event. You might believe that, because people generally don't acknowledge those they dislike, you're not a likeable person. The consequences of these actions and beliefs could be that you feel slighted and dwell on the situation. As I listened, it all seemed familiar. If I acknowledged someone and they didn't respond, I didn't consider they might simply not have seen or heard me. Instead I went straight to the default position—they didn't want to acknowledge me. I would think about the situation. Analyse it again and again, and still come out with negative feelings towards myself.

Having looked at physical tension control and relaxation previously, this session was about mental health tension control. Our facilitators reminded us although anxiety could be helpful, it might also make us think negatively. Negative thoughts could lead to avoidance. That might initially seem OK, but if left unchecked, it could mean we became more anxious. It could stop us doing something or have other people do it for us.

As I sat with others around me, I remembered my negative thoughts about driving. Causing the crash in Germany was such a stupid thing to do; how would I stop myself crashing in future? The answer? By not driving. Although I don't think I consciously decided not to drive, it was easy to make excuses so that I didn't. I had to take the train to work. It was easier for my husband to drop me at the station on his way. I realised avoiding the situation hadn't helped. It had increased my anxiety. Left me feeling less confident. Less independent. Less capable.

We learned the physical effects of anxiety compounded the negative thoughts. If we feared a situation, we might think we'd feel unwell if we experienced it. Due to the tension and anxiety we built up, we probably would feel unwell. So, afterwards, we would tell ourselves we'd been right. We thought we would feel unwell and we did. So, another barrier would go up to stop us trying again.

Hearing that negative thoughts were persuasive really struck me. My negative thoughts would just appear in my head and be totally believable. Even if they weren't based on evidence. The facilitators told us it could be difficult to dismiss negative thoughts from our minds. I certainly agreed! My negative thoughts seemed to grow and consume me until I couldn't think of anything else.

We found out we often put pressure on ourselves through unreasonable expectations. It's irrational to think you're stupid if you make one mistake. After all, everyone makes mistakes. But having this irrational belief could lead to you feeling you mustn't ever make a mistake. Let's face it: no one likes to look stupid. Using words like 'should', 'must' and 'ought' creates a judgment without us realising. One thing I was particularly aware of: I catastrophised. I made mountains out of molehills. I made things bigger than they needed to be. Often, I couldn't understand why others didn't seem to appreciate why I was so concerned. These irrational beliefs, unreasonable expectations and catastrophising often went unchallenged.

The aim of this session was to recognise our negative or faulty thoughts, then challenge them (easier said than done, I thought!). Were the thoughts correct? Were they helpful? We had to carefully consider negative thoughts and learn how to replace them with positive thoughts. The facilitators explained that if we had a difficult task ahead, we might start to think negatively about how well we would carry it out. This would cause us to feel anxious, which almost certainly meant we wouldn't do it well! Instead, we could try positive thinking. Maybe think of it as an opportunity to demonstrate how well we could do? Having positive thoughts would enable us to focus on the task at hand, without the distraction of negative thoughts.

We were reminded that how we thought directly affected the way we acted and felt. We needed to stop anxiety controlling us and instead manage our anxiety. The facilitators told us situations were rarely as bad as we thought. So what, if we made a mistake? Would the sky fall in? Would everyone notice? Would it be a disaster? What was the worst that could happen? It might be a shame, it might be inconvenient, but rarely would it result in catastrophe.

The phrase 'what's the worst that could happen?' was familiar. It's a question Mum used to ask when I was worried about something at school. Usually, as a response, we decided someone might laugh at me or I'd feel embarrassed and blush. Mum would always finish up saying, 'So, is that so bad? Isn't that something you can put up with?' Somehow, I had forgotten this technique.

Learning how to manage our anxiety, the facilitators said, put us back in charge—even if that might be hard to acknowledge. Maybe there were things we could actively do to help in certain situations, showing us we were in control of our anxiety and not in its power. I liked the idea that, by challenging my thoughts, I could affect my feelings. This meant I could do something. I didn't need to sit there while lots of negative thoughts took up residence in my brain. I was excited to think about the impact this could have. The facilitators explained we needed to practise challenging our thoughts. It was best not to procrastinate, but we needed to be reasonable too. We weren't going to solve everything immediately, and we needed to be kind to ourselves by not expecting miracles!

If we continued to think about the same worrying thing (which I recognised as a personal trait, my mind sometimes on a continuous loop, thinking the same awful thing over and over), we needed to check ourselves, allow positive thinking to begin. Just saying the word 'stop' aloud would acknowledge our decision to turn thoughts from negative to positive.

The facilitators taught us mental tension control techniques, including one based on *The Relaxation Response*.[6] For this, they advised sitting somewhere quiet in a relaxed position, focusing on the exercise. If thoughts or worries drifted in to distract us, we were to just let them go and return our attention to the exercise. We were to close our eyes, relax all our muscles from feet upwards and breathe through our noses. Every time we breathed out, we were to say the word 'one' silently to ourselves.

Ending the session, one of the facilitators said she found this exercise helpful for falling asleep at night. The word 'one' had no connection to or involvement with her thoughts. It was a neutral word. Homework for the week was to record examples of our faulty thinking and jot down how we challenged our negative thoughts with positive thinking. I found the session useful, and I looked forward to the week ahead, trying to challenge some of the catastrophising thoughts I had had.

That night as I told my husband about the session, he burst out singing. As I joined in with the second verse, it struck me a lot had changed in the past few months. I was feeling better. I was thinking again. I was looking forward to things. And I was singing with my husband, after nights and nights of him singing alone to me. As we finished, my husband said he had told me positive thinking was important. And, as usual, he was right!

One morning I saw a television interview to promote the 2011 documentary *TT3D: Closer to the Edge*. I'm not into motorbike racing and couldn't tell you the names of any riders, but it was about the Isle of Man TT races. This I knew about. At Mum and Dad's home the local television news coverage at the time spanned the border country and included the Isle of Man. Every year there would be news reports of the two-week festival, results of races and sadly, injuries and occasionally even fatalities. The motorbike racer interviewed was Guy Martin, who recounted his serious injuries in the 2010 Isle of Man TT. However, he was determined not to let that stop him racing. As I listened, I enjoyed his open, friendly and engaging style of answering and was inspired by his passion and enthusiasm. Here was someone who would not let fear of further injury dictate. He would continue doing what he loved. After allowing fear to dominate my life, I resolved to have a go at things, see how they turned out and not be concerned by the result. That night, I told my husband about the interview and the impact it had on me.

I missed seeing 'my' ambulance driver, the one who had picked me up most regularly, chatted to me as he drove and told me how cold he got in winter. I decided to knit him a hat in green to match his uniform. How to get it to him? Inspiration struck! I could ask the clinic receptionist to pass it on to him. I was sure they would manage, even though I knew only his first name. I packaged the hat, wrote a small card telling him how much he had helped me and, at my next appointment, asked the receptionist to give it to him. I was thrilled to receive a letter from him a short time later. He told me how lovely the hat was and how surprised he had been to find out there was a pressie to collect. Despite dropping hints, he said, I'd given him no clue I planned to knit for him! He was pleased he had helped me, his letter said, as he sensed I was going through a very unhappy time in my life. Although he said it was part of his job to help people, I think what he did, said and meant to me was much more than just his job.

My care co-ordinator had explained further support would be put in place for me as I reached the end of my time at the clinic. She said a staff member from another agency, which worked in the community, would meet me informally, to check in and see if I needed additional help. I thought this was a good idea and contact was made between us. We met for coffee in my hometown, although she explained she worked throughout a wider area. Although a little shy about meeting, I recognised this was nothing to do with my illness, just my nature. Soon we were talking about how far I had come and my future plans. She mentioned a weekly coffee catch-up group arranged in a nearby town and asked if I would like to attend. Some people, she explained, particularly those who lived on their own, found it helpful to have a social meeting point. I thought about it, but declined, recognising I was well-supported by my husband, neighbours and family. I wanted to develop my own network. Even though I wasn't sure how I would do this, I knew something would work out. We agreed to meet in a couple of weeks for another catch-up.

Although I usually completed the anxiety management course homework, this time I had prepared carefully written notes for the session. With the help of the cognitive behavioural therapist, I had recognised I ruminated over things. Thinking. Reliving. Becoming bogged down. Challenging my thoughts was therefore going to be important. I felt I needed to challenge the catastrophic thoughts I had experienced in the early stages of my illness. I wanted to see if I could now look at things in perspective, having had treatment from, and the support of, the clinic team.

In our circle of chairs, we began to share feedback from the previous week. I told the group I had feared I would never get well again. That had been such a constant thought, requiring me to seek reassurance from my ever-patient husband. To challenge this, I used some information I had learned from the clinic team. The professionals knew and told me I would get better. I could believe what they said because they understood my illness. Another worrying thought that had circled and circled in my mind was we would have no money because I wasn't earning. Thinking positively, I had written my husband was in a job and earning, we had some savings, we could economise and not being at work meant I had more time to shop appropriately (which meant checking prices and getting good deals). Now, telling others, it seemed hard to accept I had believed such negative, catastrophic thoughts so completely. How had I not been able to accept some logical response? I had allowed tension and anxiety to build and my negative thinking therefore fed the vicious circle, just as the facilitators had said could happen.

Another thought I had challenged was that we were going to lose our home. I had been so frightened of this, and no amount of reassurance helped. I repeated the positive challenges about earnings, savings and potential economies but also noted we could contact the mortgage company to discuss this. As I spoke, one of the facilitators reminded us not to procrastinate in situations like these. It was better to make early contact if we were concerned about our accommodation.

I challenged one final thought—that I would never relax again. All those times I had lain on my bed, the floor or sofa listening to the paper-shuffling, softly spoken woman, willing myself to relax. To let myself go. Relaxation had been elusive. I had been so busy fighting to get well that I kept winding myself up tighter and tighter. I had positively challenged the *I'll never relax again* thought by remembering I had been able to relax before (doing yoga) and it would be better not to fight the anxiety but to let it happen. I had recognised in the past, and knew now for sure, that anxiety subsided. Another challenge to that faulty thought was there were multiple forms of relaxation. If one didn't work, I could try another. My relaxation repertoire no longer consisted of only one CD; I had learned different techniques, including tai chi.

Although rooted in my past, a more recent anxiety related to driving. I explained my parents were currently visiting while my husband was overseas, and I had needed to collect them from Gatwick Airport. Despite the fun I was having driving around, my automatic thought was I couldn't pick them up by car. The road would be too busy. I wouldn't know where to go. I could go the wrong way or get lost. To challenge this, I decided if it was busy, people might drive more slowly. I had been to Gatwick before and knew its general layout, but there would also be signs, directions to the car park or pick-up point. Remembering what the facilitator had said in the last session, I asked myself, 'What's the worst that could happen?' I had decided I might not find the car park easily. If I missed it, I would drive around and try again. To laughter from the group, I explained I had indeed missed the signs to the car park. I had driven on and looped around the airport before turning back so I could try again. This time I saw the signs, parked the car and met my parents in the arrivals hall. I was so pleased with myself. I had been scared but I had still driven. I hadn't taken the train or asked my neighbour to drive. I had felt capable and independent. I had used positive thinking to challenge my worries about driving to the airport, and although it took two attempts to find the car park, who cared? The worst thing that happened? I drove around a bit more, affecting and noticed by no one. Then I laughed with my parents about missing the signs. The world didn't end. There was no catastrophe. No disaster. I was just left feeling happy that fear hadn't stopped me. The facilitator commented that fear was a much stronger emotion than disappointment. Even if I hadn't found the car park, it would have been less impactful than if I had taken the train and not challenged myself.

We continued the session, looking at the different life stresses we faced, which were different to our predecessors. We discussed how we were increasingly socially competitive ('keeping up with the Joneses') in relation to homes, appearance and status. This could lead to feelings of low self-esteem if we felt we didn't compare well to others. As many people no longer lived in the same area as their relatives, a support structure had been removed. The possibility of loneliness was introduced. As we talked, I remembered moving away from the village to the city. Gradually, I had stopped saying 'hello' to people I met in the street. I became disillusioned by the lack of acknowledgment and adopted the same strategy of non-communication.

Increasing work demands, threat of redundancy, financial pressures and awful world news events shown repeatedly were other stressors highlighted by the facilitators. The list went on. The most stressful life events, we learned, were the death of a spouse, divorce and marital separation. Life events would happen, the facilitators said. Even happy events (such as pregnancy or Christmas with the in-laws) could be stressful. They meant change. It was important to learn how to cope and adjust to the demands we would face. Sharing our feelings with others and using the practical stress-reduction tips we were learning would help us. I remembered I hadn't shared my feelings when my uncle died. I couldn't. I was slowly recognising the deep impact this had had on me.

The facilitators commented that trying to fulfil roles we thought we *should* ('good mother/father/husband/wife') could lead to stress, especially if we placed unnecessary burdens on ourselves. If we faced other demands, such as working long hours, this could create conflict. Add to the stress. They emphasised the importance of talking, rather than bottling things up. They reminded us listening was the key to good communication. We shared experiences of listening to people in our lives, recognising we had to understand them and their point of view, but we also had to understand ourselves.

Other factors that increased stress were indecision and time pressures. When facing difficult choices, we might take our time, trying to make sure we made the *right* decision. This would increase our stress levels. Making an informed decision, whatever it may be, and accepting any resulting consequences would help stress subside. We would feel better. Modern-day living meant time pressure. We were advised to use good time management techniques—planning, prioritising, delegating, using lists, saying 'no' and being realistic about what we could achieve within specific time frames.

Putting everything together, the facilitators encouraged us to identify one physical and one mental tension control technique that seemed to work for us. At our next session, we would report back on the combination of techniques we favoured. We were also to think of a stressful situation and practise controlling our anxiety levels until we stayed quite calm. I had become used to homework again, I thought, as I left the session.

It was lovely having Mum and Dad stay while my husband was away, especially since I was feeling so much better. Things were fun again. I joined in the conversation, stories and laughter as we spent time together. We talked about our family, growing up in the village and silly stories remembered from the past, which had us all chuckling. My older uncle featured in these stories. Such a lot of my early childhood seemed to include him, his wicked sense of humour and his fun. I wondered why I had had such a strong bond with him.

Mum reminded me that he was an apprentice at the village butcher's shop when I was born. Convention at that time was for shops to close on Wednesday and Saturday afternoons as well as Sunday, so staff had the equivalent of a weekend off. My uncle had his eye on the grocer's daughter. As she also had Wednesday afternoons off, he decided that would be the ideal time to try to spend time with her. He decided to suggest going a walk together and reasoned that showing up with his niece in her pram might impress her, make him seem potential husband and father material. I laughed as Mum told me this. Only my uncle could have devised a scheme involving his newborn niece as a prop to advance his prospects! Although the Wednesday-afternoon-walk-with-the-niece-in-the-pram-dates became a regular feature, apparently the grocer's daughter didn't. Things didn't work out quite as expected. My uncle thought that he was on to a winning thing, though. He continued to be a regular Wednesday afternoon babysitter while meeting, chatting up and dating other young ladies.

I was pleased to have the missing piece of the puzzle about our closeness and to find out more about him when he was younger. I liked talking about him with Mum and Dad, remembering jokes he would tell. Remembering that he always carried small packets of sugar and salt in his pocket (picked up from a café or food stall), just in case he needed it (he often did). Remembering the silly things he would do and say. Coming out of a restaurant from a family meal before the blessing of our marriage, my uncle noticed a lovely flower, which had fallen from a hanging basket. Picking it up off the ground, he inspected it before deciding it would make the perfect button-hole. He popped it in his suit jacket to complete his outfit. After the ceremony, he posed for photos, showing off his button-hole proudly as if it had been ordered specially for him. Then there was the first day of the new millennium. After our Hogmanay celebrations, which included dancing in the village square, we woke determined to walk up the hill that guarded our village. We set off with Mum brightly telling us she had brought a bottle of homemade sloe gin for a toast at the summit. Soon we were passing it around while gazing at the beautiful views surrounding us. As we left, my uncle pulled a plastic spider from his pocket. To our bemusement, he placed it on the tall stone that marks the summit. That, he said, was the Millennium Bug that everyone had been talking about. He thought it important to give it prominence on this auspicious day. Laughing and swigging sloe gin, we made our way down the hill home.

As we talked about my uncle, I remembered feeling after he passed away that the laughter in our family had died with him. I know that wasn't true. We all still laughed, but he was the joker at our gatherings. Everyone laughing at—and with—him. I felt his absence keenly. It was so nice to reminisce, to recognise the impact he had on our lives and to feel closer to him.

Mum and Dad were keen to meet my neighbours, after hearing me talk so much about them. They knew how much they were supporting me, and Dad, particularly, wanted to thank them. I had decided to invite them for a meal, and in view of the last anxiety management session, I planned to use it as my stressful situation. I felt a little anxious, particularly as my husband would usually help me; but I challenged this by thinking Mum would step in if I asked her to help. Then there were lots of things to co-ordinate. First, cooking the meal. Admittedly, I was doing better on that front but, so far, only my husband and parents had eaten what had I produced. Then I also had to make sure drinks were topped up regularly. Co-ordination hadn't been my strong point, but I thought it was improving. I was also a bit concerned about whether my neighbours would get on with Mum and Dad. My parents are very easy-going and usually have no problem meeting people. Another thought though: What if my neighbours couldn't understand Mum and Dad? Our accents are soft, and I'd never encountered problems before, but Dad was very quietly spoken.

I asked myself what was the worst that could happen. The meal would be inedible. Solution? Call a takeaway. Secondly, I might not co-ordinate the cooking times of the meal. Solution? Have a starter prepared in advance, a simple chicken dish for the main course and an easy dessert like fruit crumble. I planned the meal beforehand, thought about timings. Wrote them down in a list, identifying areas where I could delegate, deciding Mum could serve the starter. The one area I didn't try to rehearse was the Anglo-Scottish dialogue. I decided I would use the simple relaxation technique to get me through that!

I was back at the clinic for another appointment with my psychiatrist. We talked about how I was doing—how the medication was helping me, how much I had enjoyed the group activities at the clinic, how I was driving again. He asked if I visualised my endpoint when driving, and I assured him I was. It was funny how helpful that small piece of advice had been and how useful I found it in other situations.

He explained to his colleague he wanted to try something different about visualisation in this appointment and asked me if that was OK. I was happy to trust him. He had been the one to understand I didn't trust my instincts when I saw him for the first time. He had given me my own head back. He had helped me return to driving. I was interested to find out more.

He asked me to close my eyes and think about a farmyard. Easy. I immediately thought of my 'aunt's' farm where I spent holidays. I imagined myself looking out the kitchen window into the yard. I told him how the hills loomed up in front. Spring water trickled into the stone water trough at the top of the yard. Stables, barns and a workshop surrounded the yard on three sides. My psychiatrist asked me to tell him about an animal I might see there. Straight away I said a collie dog. Barrels lay on their sides along the wall of the barn to the left, and they made wonderful cosy shelters for the farmer's collies. Most of the dogs were black and white, although the farmer's favourite was a brindle colour.

Which other animal might I see? That was easy, too. A sheep. Sometimes they were brought in from the hills and fields, driven along the track and shepherded through the gate at the top right-hand corner of the yard, into the barn. Still with my eyes closed, my psychiatrist asked me to tell him about another animal there. The large black stallion, which towered over me and was stabled at the top of the yard. Although I had ridden him a few times, I found his height and size intimidating. Was there another animal in the farmyard? Yes.

I could see a goat. One of the farmer's wife's three goats. It had ambled through from its house and was picking its way through the yard. So, the psychiatrist summarised, you can see a dog, a sheep, a horse and a goat? Behind my eyelids, that's what I could see.

He asked me to open my eyes. Once I'd adjusted to the light, he handed me a sheet of paper. On it was an advertisement for a mattress company. Lying on a bed in a pair of striped pyjamas was a large cartoon hippo. I laughed as I looked. It seemed so incongruous after talking about farm animals. My psychiatrist took back the piece of paper and asked me to close my eyes again. As I did so, he asked me to think of the farmyard. What animal did I see? Without hesitation I told him that, although I wanted to say one of the farm animals, all I could see was the hippo in pyjamas! He laughed and asked me to open my eyes. We both laughed at how silly it seemed, but he explained the hippo was at the forefront of my mind. That was why I replied 'hippo'. If you think of doing something, you often end up doing it, even if it's not what you intended. It's there in your mind.

Thinking about something might mean it could happen. I could go to the kitchen to fetch an apple, but on the way there I might picture an orange. Which one would I pick up? Or I might walk into a room with a plan to put something on a table, notice a chair first and leave the room with the item happily placed on the chair. So, now I knew the potential impact of having thoughts or images at the forefront of your mind. And now you know, too. And if there's any chance you're reading this and you were the very tall, long-dark-haired male senior, who was walking down the stairs in our high school in the early 1980s, when a small girl wielding a hockey stick walked towards you, now we both know the reason for what happened that day. You see, as I approached you, I thought how awful it would be if I inadvertently hit you with my hockey stick. As we walked towards each other, my stick shot up, seemingly of its own accord. At a right angle, it walloped you in the shins! I can still see it happening. You yelled out as I hit you, seemed to jump in the air doubled over (presumably with pain, we didn't discuss it) and then seemed to leap over my stick (still suspended in mid-air) down to the bottom of the steps. I don't know who was more shocked. You yelled at me. Asked what I was doing? I couldn't explain—could only blurt out an apology. I know it's forty years later. Maybe you've forgotten about it, but I've replayed it over and over in my mind. I was so appalled that I had hurt you, even though I didn't mean it to happen. So, I'd like to apologise again. I'm very, very sorry, but at least now we both have an explanation for my actions.

I had continued to enjoy regular cranio-sacral therapy sessions. Now I took delight in driving my little car through the countryside, parking somewhere suitable and walking to the consulting rooms. It was always peaceful there—light-filled, with the faint aroma of the day's special fruit tea. After months of feeling tense, frightened and cowered in on myself, it was wonderful to recognise I felt relaxed, energised and happy, able to appreciate the lovely surroundings. My practitioner was always gentle, softly spoken and respectful, and I felt my body was beginning to respond more each session.

The occasional 'jump' of my leg would suddenly interrupt the calmness, or I would see bright colours behind my eyelids. Taking care of myself was important to me. One morning, as I arranged my next appointment, I noticed a flyer for tai chi for health. I looked more closely, excited at the prospect of being able to attend tai chi classes independently of the clinic. I remembered the careful movements. The open posture. The concentration and focus on my body as I moved. Picking up a leaflet, I resolved to find out more and see if I could join the class.

I was feeling more and more like me again. My head was a familiar, happy place. Songs and tunes replaced the heavy, dark silence. I felt I was becoming more capable, was trying new things, was being more curious and unconcerned about how things would turn out. I guess I was feeling optimistic again and freer than I had been in a long time. I was unshackled from the tortuous ruminations of my mind—acquitted of feelings of doing things wrong or not perfectly enough and liberated from the detailed planning that had accompanied my every move.

I was happy in my head. Having lost it for so long, not recognising it, I was overjoyed to feel like me again. Walking up the hill after a shopping trip one day, I was crossing the road when I realised something odd was happening to me. The happy, contented feeling left. The colours in my mind faded to blackness. I stumbled onto the pavement. Reaching for the wall, I laid my right hand flat against it to support myself. There was a buzzing sound in my head. Then it was as if someone had switched it off with a click, like I was experiencing a computer shutdown in my head. I stood there. The wall felt cool beneath my palm. I didn't know what would happen next. The silence and inactivity continued in my head as I held onto the wall and traffic passed me by. I didn't know what to do. I sensed things were OK as I was still able to think, see, hear and move. I asked myself whether my brain would restart. It seemed like minutes, but it was probably only seconds before I became aware of a clicking sound in my head. More buzzing followed. Pictures and colours appeared again. The darkness faded, tunes began to play, and it was as if nothing had happened. Cautiously I let go of the wall and, as I started to walk slowly up the hill, I wondered what had just happened.

It was our last scheduled anxiety management session, although the facilitators explained we would get together in a month to check in with each other and see how we were applying what we had learned. Feeding back on our 'homework' and, after much practice, I reported I had found the simple relaxation method to be the most effective physical relaxation technique for me, when combined with the relaxation response (breathing in and out and then saying 'one' internally) technique. Others had identified different combinations that worked for them, which just showed how individual anxiety and our responses to it were. The group laughed as I told them about rehearsing the meal for my parents and neighbours. As it turned out, the meal had been fun—lots of laughter among some serious moments when we remembered how ill I had been. I hadn't had to dial a takeaway. Success! The final part of our homework had been to list the personal goals we wanted to achieve. Goals should be practical and clear, we had been told. My list included: to drive to new and different destinations without worry, to join a tai chi class, to avoid over-rehearsing situations, and to take criticism as constructive (and an opportunity to grow and develop) rather than personally.

We started to discuss our goals, recognising sometimes we set unrealistic targets for ourselves. It might be helpful to break things down. The same applied to problem-solving. Everyone experienced problems, and negative thinking could make things worse. Looking at situations more positively could make a difference. The facilitators encouraged us to break down problems, establish facts and assumptions, and identify those parts of the problem we could control. Then they told us to think of as many solutions as possible. Nothing should be eliminated at this stage. We should then assess each solution in terms of outcome, feasibility and likelihood of success. This should result in two or three viable solutions, from which we could choose the one we liked best. We discussed using this technique on some scenarios to see how we might apply this approach to our own problems.

The facilitators then turned to irrational thinking. What did we do with our irrational thoughts? Recognised them, someone said. Challenged them, another said. The facilitators confirmed we needed to know if they were helpful, accurate and necessary. Finally, learn to replace them with positive thoughts. We looked at examples of irrational thinking. I was struck by how many had applied to me. The use of language—using words like 'should', 'must' and 'ought'—could place unreasonable demands on us. Using 'always' or 'never' could make statements more pressured, provoking us to become anxious. I was familiar with catastrophising and recognised I used statements like 'it was a total disaster' to describe something that had simply not gone as well as hoped. The facilitators suggested we try to be more realistic, to ask ourselves if the situation was really that bad. They introduced 'all or nothing thinking' and gave the example of one thing going wrong. We might say, 'Everything's going wrong, the whole day is going to be like this'. Did I do this? Guilty! Instead, we were encouraged to take note of when we did this and remember no one was perfect. A-ha! As my husband continued to remind me, I was Imperfect Perfect; I could relate. When the next one—Negative selection/Discounting the positive—was read out, I felt like throwing my hand in the air and yelling 'House' as if at bingo. I did this too! I looked at myself and noticed negative factors. I ignored the positives and counted them as unimportant. The tip from the facilitators was to recognise when we discounted ourselves, notice when we did things well and give ourselves credit. I thought back to the volunteer driver who had asked me to remain beautiful. Despite my usual traits, I hadn't protested—hadn't tried to downplay what he said, hadn't tried to minimise a lovely compliment. His words had touched me. In future, I resolved to thank people if they paid me a compliment.

It seemed positive thinking and a sense of humour would help me with negative thinking. I had rediscovered my sense of fun and decided to apply it whenever I had negative thoughts. As we left the session, we were given another handout on improving our social life. I remembered going to a work function with my husband the summer before I was ill. As I stood there, among the others, I realised I had no conversation. Nothing to say. Nothing of interest. Looking over the handout, I recognised I probably looked anxious, walking with rounded shoulders, head bent over. I possibly looked tense. I knew I didn't make eye contact with people around that time. Maybe I gave off vibes to indicate people should keep away? Being shy, I tended not to like social gatherings overly much, but I was reassured to read that people generally valued a good listener, rather than a sparkling conversationalist. I could listen. I could show my interest in what someone was saying by nodding and using facial expressions to show I was following what they said. I could add comments or ask questions. Thinking back to the recent dinner I'd attended with my husband, when I had taken my homemade fruit-loaf, I remembered that although I'd been nervous, I'd listened. Contributed. Had fun. I decided, though, in future I needed to be able to talk about something other than work.

It seemed hearing the phrase 'what's the worst that can happen?' had triggered memories of good advice that, perhaps, I hadn't paid enough attention to over my adult life. Now I remembered not only that advice, but who had given it to me. Never look in windows (that was Dad, conscious about people's privacy); life's too busy to dust (that was Mum, who took her own advice seriously); toilet rolls should always be placed to roll over the holder (that from Gran, a tip from her days as a maid, when she learned rolling under the holder meant the backs of hands might touch the wall and leave greasy marks). Just some of the advice I remembered, but not quite so impactful as other advice I received. Look all around you at the wonders of nature. That was both Mum and Gran, who wanted us to see the beauty surrounding us. Always defend yourself, but never make the first move. This was from Dad again. He instilled in us that if someone went for us physically, we should respond as hard as we could, with everything we had. We would be assured of his wholehearted support. If we attacked first, we were on our own.

Mum and Dad had been careful not to burden my sister and me with expectations. While others in my class at school were rewarded monetarily if they did well in their exams, Mum and Dad told us, 'Just do your best'. Always followed by, 'If you've done your best, that's all you can do, there's nothing more'. How sensible. It meant I went into exams, races and job interviews with only one goal in mind: just to do my best. It gave me freedom, although I don't think I realised that at the time. The words would stay with me, like a comfort blanket. I knew in any given situation I had to try to do my best and then, irrespective of the outcome, I could be satisfied there was nothing more I could do.

So how had I forgotten 'Just do your best'? How had I become fixated on perfection? When had it started? I'm not sure. I wasn't aware of it. There was nothing to suggest I was striving for perfection; it just seemed to happen. When I ran the clinical assessment centre for doctors from overseas, I was responsible for an important exam. We had to make sure it was consistent for all candidates, that it was run without fault, to allow every doctor to demonstrate their skills and abilities. Had I somehow allowed this aim for excellence, this intent to run the ideal exam, this objective to produce the consummate experience, to spill over into other aspects of my life? I don't know. But hearing the words 'Just do your best' took me back to times when I didn't scrutinise everything and criticise myself for shortcomings.

My first long-term boss, a large man with a gentle nature and a booming voice (which served him well as a sergeant-major in the Territorial Army) also passed on some wise words. He was aware he could descend into internal conversation with himself over a situation. He would reflect on it, then start to analyse it more deeply from several different viewpoints. He would begin to imagine how he would handle it and would speculate on conversations he would have with people. 'First I'll say this . . . then they'll respond that . . . then I'll answer them with this . . ..' Being aware of these tendencies, he knew to stop himself and make sure that, while analysing and preparing, he didn't overdo it. He cautioned me how such conversations could lead to making judgments (often wrong) about people, attributing words and statements they might never utter, and bestowing them with particular behavioural styles which might be entirely inappropriate.

So how, given this sage advice, had I reached the stage where I entered conversations having thought out, practised, practically rehearsed the exchange as I anticipated it? How had I let myself become worked up about situations that might never arise? How had I gone beyond the initial preparatory stage of determining information I might need, straight into the imaginary discussion itself. I can't tell you. I don't know. I was spending time and energy on things that didn't need it. One thing I have recognised, I'm very thorough. No matter what I'm doing—hoovering, making arrangements, weeding—I'm thorough. Maybe this whole internal dialogue was an attempt to cover all bases? Whatever was behind it, I decided enough was enough. Having recognised it, it wouldn't happen again. I planned to adopt the same strategy as my boss, keeping a check on preparations.

Then there was the advice from our dance teacher (we'd taken classes early in our marriage), a small bird-like lady, light on her feet and so wispy a strong gust of wind would surely carry her away. She had the unenviable task of trying to teach our small group (which included a couple who danced in Dr. Martens and another with nervous flatulence problems) ballroom and Latin American dance in a little school hall. Eschewing modern CDs and players, she brought in her trusty cassette recorder each week. The tapes must have been played over and over thousands of times. My husband and I would listen expectantly for those few, brief seconds of recording malfunction in the quickstep when the music stopped and silence (apart from the heavy thud of Dr. Martens) reigned. On learning we were not able to continue classes due to my husband's increasing workload, she told us it was important to have things in life other than work.

So how had my life turned into a cycle of sleep, work, eat, repeat? How had I dropped activities and hobbies I used to enjoy and simply gone to work and come home again? I've no idea. I think again it was a gradual thing. I had a fairly long commute to work and once I was home, I couldn't be bothered to do much more than make a meal and watch television. Weekends were for catching up on housework, sleeping and visiting family or friends. I just stopped making the effort to be involved, and I wanted that to change.

After setting a personal goal to join a tai chi class and finding the flyer at the cranio-sacral therapy session, I telephoned the number for more information. Beginners classes were due to start in early May in the town where I would be working. How perfect was that? I could finish work and then go to the class. I was thrilled at the prospect. The advice from the cognitive behavioural therapist was still fresh in my mind: 'Please remember to maintain a work–life balance, as this will stand you in good stead for the future'. I was committed to making sure work was not going to be my sole focus in future. Thanks to the staff at the clinic and everyone who had looked after me, I had been given the chance to be healthy, free and independent. I was determined to enjoy all the possibilities opening up to me.

A few weeks before restarting work, I drove past white chalk cliffs to my first tai chi class. I was driving a new route. Just because I could. I had prepared—worked out where it would be held and identified my route. Visualised my endpoint—parking in the car park close to the studio. The door was locked and, as I was a little early, I waited outside, striking up conversation with some others who arrived. A man cycled up, dismounted and greeted us all, telling us he would lead the class. Up some stairs, we entered a long room with large skylights, enabling us to see the roofs of houses and properties around us. He introduced himself and asked each of us to give our name and how much tai chi we had done before. I was happy to say my name and that I'd done a small amount, so I was a beginner. I didn't feel I wanted to share more details about my introduction to tai chi.

Wearing loose-clothing as instructed, we spread out through the studio, so we had enough room to swing our arms without hitting the next person. The instructor proceeded to show us warm-up exercises, focusing on different areas throughout the body. Some I was familiar with; others were new. Some needed concentration and balance; others didn't. While telling us more about tai chi and its health benefits, the teacher showed us how to walk softly, hardly putting weight on his foot as he stepped forward. Transferring to his other leg, he told us shifting our bodyweight was important in tai chi. We did some exercises, being encouraged to move smoothly, not to have rigid arms or legs and to notice our posture. As we followed, trying to make our movements resemble those of our teacher, I remembered how much I had enjoyed the gentle repetition of tai chi and the concentration it required. I was pleased I had found a way to continue practising it outside the clinic.

As I was returning to work soon, I wanted to visit my family. I flew up, again with a small bag, but this time with a smile on my face, feeling happy. My parents were waiting to collect me and soon I was back in the village and setting off to visit Gran. Later, Mum and

I walked down the waterside. Although we hadn't talked much about the night I'd put myself in the river, I found myself telling her about running in the moonlight. I explained I knew how far along the path I had come because of the smell of wild garlic, which grew in a clump under the trees. Mum asked me about this. Was I sure it was wild garlic? Yes, definitely. It was such a familiar smell at that location. Mum shrugged, explaining wild garlic didn't flower in September, so there wouldn't be any aroma. It was odd. We continued to walk as I puzzled over this. The smell had been so pervasive, so vivid, so real. It was only later I put two and two together. After being prescribed anti-psychotic medication, I had gone online to find out more about psychosis. I thought people who were psychotic were violent. That seemed to be a myth. Vulnerable was probably more appropriate. Symptoms of psychosis included seeing, hearing, feeling, tasting or smelling something that wasn't there. Even though I smelled wild garlic, it wasn't there. I was amazed. I've never gambled, but I would have bet everything I own on being able to smell wild garlic that night.

Mum, Dad and my sister all commented how different I was, compared to my last stay in December. I joked with them, laughed with them, delivered little one-liners. I did things, I suggested things, I participated in things. I was me again. Sitting round the table at breakfast, tablets on the placemats in front of us (some things hadn't changed), Dad said how wonderful it was to see me back. I knew what he meant. He had told Mum for a long time that something didn't seem right with me. When I left after each visit, he'd think I'd lost my vitality, my spark, my bubbly nature. He didn't understand it, couldn't quite put his finger on what it was. Even if he had mentioned it to me, it wouldn't have made a difference. I didn't see it. I couldn't see it; there was nothing tangible there for me to pick up. We agreed it didn't matter; we were looking forward with smiles on our faces.

It was time to re-read 'The Rules of Assertion'. After months of carrying the small card in my wallet, I wanted to read it again: 'I have the right to respect myself—who I am and what I do.' I was me— Ali Plus. I was happy, joyful, caring, protective of others, assertive, determined, a bit cookie, hard-working, curious. I knew who I was again. I could look back over the months of illness—the struggle to get better—and see me emerging through it all. I continued to read:

'Recognise my own needs as an individual.' I did now. I needed to be connected to family and friends, involved with something other than work and feel I made a difference. I recognised I had become completely insular, cutting myself off, allowing none of myself to be seen by others.

'Make clear 'I' statements about how I feel and what I think.' I was able to. All the work with psychiatrists and therapists had needed me to reflect and talk about me. I had realised my tendency to couch instructions at work as 'we' statements: 'We should do this in that way'. I asked staff to carry out tasks in an indirect way, making suggestions as a collective rather than owning my personal ideas. Now it would be different in both my work and home lives. I would say what I wanted to happen—what I needed others to do, what I thought was best.

The next rule was 'Allow myself to make mistakes.' I had started to. My husband telling me to aim for imperfect perfection had helped more than he realised. I remembered a mistake at work. After confessing to my boss, explaining what I was doing to correct it, she commented how quickly I had reacted. Everyone makes mistakes, she told me; what matters is recognising them, putting them right and learning from them. I would remember her words in future. I wouldn't beat myself up if I got something wrong. 'Change my mind, if I choose', I read. Had I had a problem with changing my mind in the past? I wasn't sure, but this rule gave me reassurance, confidence it was OK to admit I'd thought things over and reconsidered.

The next rule was 'Ask for 'thinking it over time'.' Before I was ill, I had felt clear and confident about the next steps I would take. Something inside had told me what to do. Maybe instinct? Over the time my head had been silent, I hadn't had that instant response. I couldn't make decisions quickly and had discovered it wasn't necessary. Sometimes it was good not to be rushed, to recognise further time to think and reflect was needed.

Number seven was 'Allow myself to enjoy my successes.' I had learned to do this. Whether it was something written in the creative writing class or knitted or something I had painted in the art class, I'd learned to give myself a pat on the back. I knew I had brushed off compliments before. Even as a child when Mum said I'd done something well, I shrugged my shoulders. When managers praised my work, I just thought I was doing my job. I minimised positive feedback. Well, no more. I would enjoy it.

'Ask for what I want' was the next rule—probably the one I had most difficulty with. I'd been brought up to say, 'I'd like . . .'. It was impolite to say what you wanted. 'I want never gets' was a regular refrain from Gran. I'd also learnt from Gran to put others first. When she took me, my sister and younger cousins on holiday, we were treated to cakes she'd chosen at the bakers—all different. Each day there were six small cakes. Some were chocolate, others cream or fruit. I watched as she offered the box round, so we could each choose. Gran would always take the last one; she never chose. I modelled myself on this, putting others first. So, I knew this was the rule I was going to find hardest to exercise.

'Recognise that I am not responsible for the behaviour of other adults.' I wasn't. I knew that. I had invited teachers, pupils and co-workers from my summer job in the local furniture factory (I'd been responsible for cupboard door handles and hinges) to a party before I left Germany. My landlord had asked how I would feel if someone drank alcohol, then had an accident driving home. I told him I was arranging a party. Alcohol would be available. It was up to guests to decide whether they drank, how much and what method of transport they used to go home. So although I knew I wasn't responsible, it was helpful to have this rule as reinforcement.

The next rule was 'Respect other people and expect the same in return.' I did. I had been brought up to be respectful. I used the titles of the doctors and professors I'd worked with. I was careful about the privacy of others. Polite to everyone I interacted with. Mum and Dad had insisted that we 'treat others the way you'd wish to be treated'. They had set an example which I followed.

The penultimate rule was 'Say I don't understand.' Hmmm. That one took more thought. I wasn't sure if I'd had a problem in saying this before. I recognised though, this rule granted permission not to understand something and to be open about it. Finally, 'Deal with others without being dependent on them for approval.' I did. Possibly because Mum had instilled in me that I was my own person, an individual. I wasn't concerned about what others thought of me. At school we had gone to a schoolboy's international rugby match in winter. Mum and Gran made sure I was wrapped up in a long coat and boots. I was aware of whispered comments as we got off the bus: 'What on earth is she wearing?', 'What does she look like?' They didn't bother me; I was snug as we huddled in the stands, the wind blowing coldly around us.

So, I'd got to the end of the ten rules. Unlike the first time I'd read them, I was able to think about them, challenge myself and see where I needed to focus my attention. It had been a useful exercise.

Things were moving ahead with work. I had met my existing and new line manager to catch up on developments since I'd been away and to find out more about the transfer of the service to the new directorate. A lot had changed in the months I had been absent, but other things were still the same! Now I was back in my employer's headquarters for another meeting with my old and new managers and a personnel officer. This one focused on my impending return to work. Even though I was driving regularly on my own, I decided to meet my employment specialist so we could travel together. As she drove, we chatted about having a new manager, a new work location and, essentially, a new start.

My manager had just received a report from the Occupational Health doctor. My employment specialist and I were given a copy so we could discuss it during the meeting. She recommended a six-week phased return to work, starting with four-hour sessions, two mornings each week. She noted I would benefit from continued management support and flexibility, from regular management review and being provided with feedback. The tasks I was to be given during my phased return were to be considered carefully, with the complexity of tasks gradually increasing during the six-week period. My employment specialist asked if I was happy with the proposed schedule. As I had no point of reference, I confirmed I would be guided by the experience of the Occupational Health doctor.

I updated my new manager that I was feeling ready to return to work. I was happy and excited to return and expected to be declared medically fit in early June, following appointments with both my psychiatrist and general practitioner. My new manager proposed the interim manager should continue in the role. This would provide me with support and ensure I could do as much as I was able to, without feeling undue pressure. I would work in an office with other staff from a similar public-facing service. It might also be helpful to plan some short visits to the four registration offices before my formal return. I agreed; I was pleased with all these arrangements. After determining a time to meet on my first day, we arranged I would contact my new manager after meeting my psychiatrist. I thanked my managers for their support and allowing me time to concentrate on my recovery. I was grateful to them both, old and new, for their thoughtful care. As we drove back, my employment specialist and I remarked on how much had changed since our first meeting in early January. I hadn't been sure then that I would ever be able to work again.

Although I had attended only a few tai chi sessions, I would miss the next one. My husband and I were taking a short holiday in Malta. I had made the arrangements, noting travel insurance wouldn't cover my pre-existing medical condition, but feeling confident a combination of medication and all I had learned would mean an incident-free week. At the hotel we received a warm welcome and, in our room, found a card addressed to me with a bottle of champagne. We looked at each other. Had my husband told them about my illness and subsequent recovery? No. Had Mum and Dad somehow arranged the surprise? If not, who? Did everyone get this welcome? We agreed I would have only a small celebratory glass, mindful of instructions not to drink alcohol when taking medication. Next day we explored, walking through streets, admiring views, enjoying our time together in the sun. Arriving back in our room, we found no bottle of champagne. Instead, flower petals were scattered across the bed, a box of chocolates lay on the table and a card addressed to me was propped up against it. The message inside said the staff hoped I was enjoying my stay. We didn't understand. Who would have arranged this? I decided to find out why I was receiving gifts and asked my husband to accompany me downstairs. The receptionist was pleased I enjoyed my gifts, but queried why I thought they weren't for me. She checked with a colleague, before confirming they were intended for someone else—a senior executive of the hotel chain, coincidentally, with the same name and travel dates! She had cancelled her booking at the last minute. The staff hadn't realised because of my booking. Glad to have the puzzle solved, we continued to enjoy our holiday and the chocolates.

CHAPTER 8

June–August 2011 – Return

My psychiatrist had arranged to see me for a final check before I went back to work—just to make sure I felt ready, he said. I was amazed at how much had changed since our first appointment. He had been spot-on with the medication he prescribed, had got to know me and my foibles, and had taught me so much about myself. I was excited but nervous about returning to work. How would I feel? How would people treat me? Would I cope? There was one thing, above all, I was concerned about. What would happen if I encountered the same situation as before? What if no words came? If the screen stayed blank? The image, only 'Funeral Celebrant Interviews' at the top, had stayed with me. My psychiatrist said he was confident that wouldn't happen. If it did, what would I do? I sat for the briefest of seconds before answering, 'Take a deep breath and picture the endpoint I want to reach'. Under his careful guidance I had learned everything else would fall into place. I would see myself sitting at a computer screen, typing away until I had finished the document. I would get there.

Six weeks after our last session and the day before I returned to work, I attended the final session of our anxiety management course. It was nice to see other group members, and we were keen to catch up. 'Have you used the panicking penguin yet?' I asked the lady who had nicknamed the emergency relaxation technique. Due to the arm flapping, it will always be the 'panicking penguin' to me. She giggled, telling us about a situation where she had used it. Soon everyone in the group was laughing.

Each of us provided an update, including what we thought of the course. I said I was returning to work next day and received

162

congratulations. From the in-drawn breaths of people around me, I could tell they thought it a big thing. I felt a mixture of excitement and nervousness, I said, but I recognised that was normal. The course had been very useful, and I had learned so much—not just from the facilitators, but also the other participants. I told them my personal crusade was to avoid using the word 'should' and that, if I did, I would check myself and find another way to express myself. I felt pleased to tell them about joining a tai chi class; I was achieving a personal goal. When asked about driving, I explained I had driven to the scheduled informal visits at registration offices. I no longer worried about parking. Gone were the days of reversing back and forward to make sure the car was straight.

As I reflected on the course, I remembered and shared the piece of information that had the most impact on me. In the early sessions we found out about the two different branches of the autonomic nervous system. Learning that the branch which worked to calm us down could not do so if the other 'fight or flight' branch was activated was a game-changer for me. I realised I was not powerless, was not at the mercy of anxiety. But I didn't need to fight it. I needed to learn to relax.

After listening to the others, the facilitators gave us one final handout, to help us remember what we had learned about physical and mental tension control. We had covered a lot—appreciating anxiety was normal, identifying our stress positions, recognising early-warning signs, applying relaxation in everyday tasks, and remembering that exercise was a healthy way to release tension. We had learned a lot too—how faulty thinking caused anxiety, avoidance increased anxiety and anxiety subsided, so it was best to stay with it. The facilitators congratulated us on completing the course and reminded us our achievements were a result of our own hard work. I clutched my handout, enjoying my success as 'The Rules of Assertion' stated, as we left for the last time.

My first day back at work was strange: A new office location. A different drive to work. Not a full day. The Occupational Health doctor had said I could expect to be very tired when I resumed work. Eight months after I left, I returned. After meeting my manager and the interim manager, I was taken to the open-plan office where I would work. I recognised a familiar face. One of the two colleagues from my last day, who had taken on the organisation of the funeral celebrant interviews. She hugged me tightly and said how good it was to see me. Then she asked me to choose one of two desks. Feeling slightly self-conscious but remembering 'The Rules of Assertion', I asked for the one I wanted—by the window. I met the other office occupants and settled down to work. My manager had told me to delete all the emails in my inbox. Good news! I had had visions of wading through a slew of information, not knowing which messages still had currency. The interim manager would forward any relevant ones.

At lunchtime, my manager came to make sure I was taking a break. Carrying my lunch, I left to go for a short walk. Wandering down the hill, I noticed a small seat, built into a wall—the perfect place to sit in the sun to eat lunch. After a few minutes, I realised I had come to the crescent. On that Friday before my meltdown, this was where my mind suddenly sped up, where thoughts had started to slam into my head. Would being here affect me? Take me back to that day? To how I felt? No. I recognised where I was, but cocooned in the warmth of the wall, I enjoyed my lunch, looking out over the roofs below, watching as people went about their business. After a short break I returned to the office, feeling refreshed from the outside air. Much better than my previous practice of eating at my desk. I spent the rest of my first 'day' back meeting colleagues and catching up on progress. Soon I was in my car, bouncing through the country lanes on my way home for a snooze. The Occupational Health doctor had been right; I was tired!

Over the next two weeks, I gradually became more familiar with what was going on and got to know my new office-mates. It was lovely to be with people again, to be in the work environment again. I enjoyed quick chats while making tea or coffee. I felt comfortable with my new manager. I realised she was keeping an eye on me, but it was done in a supportive manner. She would pop in to make sure I was having a lunch break away from my desk. Let me know if she was heading out the office for meetings. Comment on the plant I had placed on the windowsill next to my desk. I wasn't sure what the staff had been told about my return. Did they know what had happened to me? Was there speculation about my illness? No one said anything to me about it. No one asked questions. People told me how nice it was to see me back, how well I looked. One colleague sent an email saying he thought I looked happy. How great it was to see. He was right. I was happy. But I was very relieved not to have to answer questions about my time off. It meant I could focus on the future, not dwell on the past.

Occasionally I had lunch with colleagues in the café at work, deep in the bowels of the building. I made sure I continued to have a break, aware I felt fresher in the afternoon. One day, as I finished eating, I noticed the Occupational Health doctor join the queue. Although I hadn't seen her since our last meeting, I was fairly sure it was her. I told my friends I would join them outside and approached her. As I'm renowned for my inability to recognise faces, I checked first it was her. I reminded her who I was, then thanked her for the care and help she'd given me. She looked surprised. I reminded her she had warned me I would be tired on my return. She had been right! I also said the phased return had been critical for me. I left her in the queue with a large smile on her face. I felt good telling her how much her help had meant to me.

When we drew up my traffic light plan, my care co-ordinator suggested it was important to have some significant items that could lift me, if I felt down. It took me a while to get my mental health first aid kit together. I wanted to work out what was most important to me. On my most recent stay with Mum and Dad, we had gone with my aunt to lay flowers at my uncle's grave. In the sunshine at the top of the hill, I was able to share how I felt on the day of his funeral, how devastated when we missed his burial. Now I felt peace, knowing I had acknowledged the important part he played in my life. Later, I noticed my aunt displayed, amongst others, a picture of my uncle and me. It was taken at my big cousin's wedding. It showed his lovely smile, sitting with a pint in front, with me looking at him, laughing at something he said. I asked my aunt for a copy, so I could look at it when I wanted. It is so special to see us having fun together. My kit also contains knitting magazines, some wool and needles. Mum continues a subscription to a knitting magazine for me. I love to look at all the colourful designs, try some of the patterns, and read about other knitters and their projects. I find knitting relaxing. I enjoy the repetitive movements that produce hats, toys, blankets and more. There is also a blessing bowl in my kit, a small handmade bowl in brown and gold, the colour calling out to me when I saw it. Inside it, written on a small piece of paper, are the things I am most grateful for: my health, my husband, my family and my happiness. I learned how important my health is, how not to take it for granted. Every time I pass the bowl, I am reminded to look after myself and be grateful for my continuing good health, the people I hold most dear and my happiness.

Although my involvement with the clinic had lessened significantly (I now only attended for appointments), I was asked to help with interviews for an occupational therapist. A patient representative was needed to provide a different perspective. The clinic team knew I had taken part in interviews before. It seemed both an opportunity to give back to the people who had supported me and to help those who would come after me—those who needed help like me. I was introduced as a patient of the clinic, someone who had used its services and was nearing a transfer back to general care. I found it interesting meeting candidates, finding out about their experience and, from my perspective, seeing how they would engage with potential patients. I was happy with the final choice, confident they would continue the wonderful care I had received.

After attending the anxiety management course and reflecting on signs that had precipitated my illness, I had become more attuned to recognising stress in others. One day I became aware a colleague in our shared office was having a difficult and frustrating telephone conversation. His posture stooped. His arms and shoulders tensed. His tone of voice belied irritation. He terminated the conversation, explaining he needed to move to a private office to continue the discussion.

I watched as he moved, noticing he appeared disheartened and unhappy. I boiled the kettle, made a cup of tea and, not knowing what he liked in it, took some milk and sugar. I knocked on the door, quietly went in and laid the tea, milk and sugar before him. He looked up and smiled a thanks. His shoulders visibly dropped from his ears and, instantly, he looked more relaxed. Making a cuppa was a small thing. I know it didn't help his difficult telephone conversation, but it gave him a breather and showed him that we looked out for each other.

Before resuming full-time work, two months after last seeing him, I had another appointment with my psychiatrist. In the waiting room, I reflected that the clinic no longer seemed so familiar. A woman came in to wait for someone attending an appointment. She recognised another woman in the waiting room, who looked grey and unwell. Together they talked quietly; the second woman became upset, rocking back and forward in her seat. The woman continued to speak in a low, soothing voice before gradually putting her arms round the second woman, holding her tightly. I was called to my appointment and left the two of them, sitting hugging in the waiting room. I remembered all the times I'd needed the comfort of my husband's arms—times when words couldn't reach me. Reassurance meant nothing. The relief of being held, being safe, was something I could appreciate.

My psychiatrist was keen to know about my return to work. I happily told him how great I felt. I was able to concentrate and remember (although I wrote lists frequently), and things were going well. We talked about my phased return and he acknowledged the tiredness I had felt, although he was pleased that I was beginning to feel more energised. Was I driving? I laughed with him as I told him there was no stopping me! I'd driven to three offices rather than travelling by train, and I was pleased with myself. He questioned how I prepared for these trips. I explained about making sure I knew the route, leaving plenty of time so I didn't feel under pressure if there was heavy traffic and about focusing on my endpoint. I visualised myself parking at the destination. He asked if that was working for me, and I laughingly reassured him it was. I would never have thought his advice could make so much difference. Had I experienced having a blank sheet of paper and not being able to write anything? He said he knew I worried about this. No. Although the memory of the experience was vivid, it was a memory. The present saw me open documents on the computer, think about what I wanted to write and then type away. I told him about my new line manager, my new office location and my office-mates. He was happy things had changed for me and I no longer felt isolated. I would have one follow-up appointment in about a month, he said, but he fully expected I would then be discharged from specialist care. He was really pleased with my progress. I left the clinic with a spring in my step.

As we had agreed, I attended some appointments with the counsellor throughout my phased return. I felt different in the sessions with her. I was confident, chatty, happy—not cowering in my seat, feeling overwhelmed. I was able to think about and reflect on my experience and was comfortable talking about it. I told the counsellor I had rediscovered who I was, explaining the story Mum had told me about 'being me' before I was anything to anyone else. The counsellor commented it was a wonderful thing for a mother to tell her daughter and a very empowering statement. I hadn't equated the word 'empowered' with the story, but I recognised how right she was.

In my first week of full-time work I faced a test, chairing a meeting, the first since I had returned. To be fair, it was a small meeting of the managers and training co-ordinator, but I was still nervous. Would I remember things? Would I be able to co-ordinate the agenda, note-taking and chairing? Would there be any reaction to the way I chaired it? The interim manager, who was returning to her substantive post, kindly offered to support me at the meeting. I had found her to be a lovely person—open, warm and an ideal mentor as she helped my transition to leading the team again. We gathered in one of the registration offices and I began the meeting. I asked one of the managers to take notes, rather than trying to do it myself. Although I felt a bit self-conscious as I introduced items, I soon felt as if I was getting into the swing of things. When acknowledging suggestions and comments, I began to say 'Thank you, that's a really valuable contribution'.

The meeting continued. I began to feel more assured. I was able to remember things, I could connect comments being made with things I knew, I acknowledged what people said and I was able to ask for background information when discussing issues that had arisen while I was off. 'Thank you, that's a really valuable contribution', I repeated after one manager's comments, noticing some of the team look at each other when I did so. I decided to shake things up a bit (remembering the counsellor's words), making sure I showed appreciation with different words and phrases. I was doing it! I was back at work, involved in the service again and leading my team. Who would have thought it?

Later that afternoon I sought feedback from my mentor on the meeting and my leadership of it. She gave feedback, answered some queries and then paused, before saying, 'To be honest, we were just thankful that you stopped saying "Thank you, that's a really valuable contribution" every time someone spoke.' Together we laughed as I explained I had (finally!) realised how often I was saying the words. I didn't take it as criticism. I was just grateful for her direct, although kindly said, response.

In mid-August, after almost a month of full-time work, I had my final review at the clinic. It seemed funny to be back in what had been almost my second home. My care co-ordinator remarked how relaxed I looked. I could only agree. I was feeling wonderful. The shaky legs and buzzing feeling were a distant memory. The vacantness in my head seemed almost impossible to recollect. I felt bright, bubbly and happy as I told my care co-ordinator about returning to full-time work. I was enjoying work again and was also doing things outside work. How did I feel about being discharged back to the care of my general practitioner? A little nervous, I said, although I felt the time was right and I had a whole host of resources to keep me well. My care co-ordinator agreed, saying I had made a significant and continued recovery since our first contact before Christmas. She would forward a copy of my traffic light plan to my doctor and the team would be happy to see me again if needed. Although I had thought I would see my psychiatrist for the review, it seemed fitting that my first and last interaction with the specialist support services team was with my care co-ordinator.

Now back at work, I was conscious of making sure my life was balanced. I enjoyed the tai chi classes I was attending; in summer they were outside, which was lovely. Coincidentally, they were held in the beautiful gardens next to the registration office! But I wanted something more. My husband and I registered for a car boot sale and found ourselves in the middle of a large car-park with the boot of my little silver car open, selling our unwanted wares. Later in the morning a man wearing a high-visibility vest came to the unopened car next to us and began to set items out. We chatted and I learned he was a member of the organising charity, Rotary International. He told me about Rotary, which I knew a little about since Mum had given talks in her role as a Stroke Charity co-ordinator at local meetings. I wanted to contribute to my local community so decided to find out more.

After meeting several members and attending some weekly meetings, I joined the local club. I got to meet new people, participate in local events, feel connected. With other members I carried out mock interviews for school leavers, giving them an opportunity to identify and verbalise their skills and achievements. I helped with a public-speaking competition for high-school students, listening as they confidently spoke on their assigned topics, before asking questions to check their understanding. I helped fund-raise, collecting money in local shopping centres, and raising the profile of the charity in the community. I felt I was not only giving back, but I was learning too. I learned how much I had missed public speaking, for one thing. Despite years of enjoyment, feeling energised by it, feeling confident about it, I had shut myself down after one presentation I felt didn't go well. But in the kind company of the Rotary Club, I found myself speaking in front of others, thanking guest speakers and giving presentations. I found my voice again.

CHAPTER 9

September 2011 to Date – This is Me Now

Some things have changed since my breakdown. One of the most significant is that my husband and I now live in Australia. He was offered a senior position at a university in Melbourne and so watching episodes of *Wanted Down Under* was put to good use! Eighteen months after I returned to work, we moved across the world. Far from that first creative writing class at the clinic, when I feared we would never travel again, we enjoy exploring a new country and continent.

In the speech she gave at my leaving party, my manager said it had been quite surreal taking over responsibility for the service, because she didn't get to know me for a few months. Although we had only worked together for a relatively short time, she thought we made a formidable partnership and was miffed my husband had the audacity to get a job overseas! From my perspective, I had really enjoyed working with her. We tackled issues facing us, developed relationships both within and outwith the organisation, and were praised for our leadership. My manager was someone who got to know me well, who was supportive without being overbearing and who recognised my peculiar foibles— and then challenged them. In one meeting she encouraged me not to make the issue we were discussing bigger than it was! See, despite everything, I still sometimes tended to favour mountains over molehills.

Before moving I was aware that I needed to plan for my on-going good health, so I discussed this with my doctor. I knew moving ranked as one of the top five most stressful life events. Besides all the preparation and organisation, there would also be meeting new people, living in a new area and becoming accustomed to a different way of life. Together we made the decision that I would continue with both the anti-psychotic and anti-depressant medication, until I was settled in my new home. As we needed medical examinations before moving, I was prepared to disclose my illness and treatment but did not know what to say. How would I describe what had happened? Although I used the term 'nervous breakdown' (it indicated not knowing what had happened) I realised these words were not used by the medical profession. Instead they referred to anxiety and depression. The Occupational Health doctor at work had referred to 'a serious psychiatric condition'. My psychiatrist had reassured me I was unlikely to have a recurrence, especially as I had learned so much during treatment, but I was concerned that my illness might count against me. Being able to describe it properly in the medical examination was important to me. Discussion with my doctor was helpful. She clarified I had experienced a severe depressive episode, for which I continued to take medication, but this would be reviewed once I was established in my new situation. It was helpful to have her insight, as well as my medical records, when I went for the medical exam. Interestingly, I found the authorities were more interested in whether I had tattoos or varicose veins than about my mental health.

I moved to my new home armed with copies of my medical records, so I could pass them on to my new general practitioner. I looked for a doctor with an interest in mental health and was delighted to find someone who was empathetic and practical. We planned my slow reduction and withdrawal from the anti-psychotic medication, a significant step. Following my illness, I had viewed it as a one-off—something that had happened, but from which I had recovered. Not ongoing. I felt well-armed with my traffic light plan, the information about anxiety management and the work–life balance I had worked hard to achieve. I knew I was not invincible. Still I was not prepared for what followed.

As part of establishing our financial affairs in a new country, we considered life assurance. Our adviser sent us application forms to complete. I had the necessary medical information ready, including dates and treatment and so started to fill out the form. I came to the last question: 'Have you ever tried to kill yourself?'

Although I had told them about it, I had never discussed the river episode with my doctor, psychiatrist or therapists. Only the psychiatrist in Scotland had asked, 'Alison, why did you try to harm yourself last night?'

I had not answered her, had not known. Later in my treatment I had been glad not to question it—instead, I wanted to focus on the future.

Now, reading those blunt words, I had to confront it. Had I? I remembered that night. Being on the phone with my husband. Him asking what would happen next. I had not known. I had run. Flown. Sought solace in the river to try to stop the thoughts that hit my head so hard. My fight or flight response was to flee. Was I trying to kill myself? I knew I had thought about how the river had taken people away. Their bodies found further downstream in the days and weeks that followed. I had looked at the river as I crossed the bridge. Noticed it was high. Running faster than normal. Considering all this, maybe I had.

Surely, I would have felt more emotion, though? Surely trying to kill yourself involved more than slipping into a river under the cover of darkness? It was as if it had happened to someone else. I could see what was happening but did not understand the motivation. I knew I wanted the thoughts to stop slamming into my head. Stop them hurting me. I was aware of nothing else. Sometimes such actions are said to be a cry for help, attention-seeking. None of those thoughts hit my head that night. Only, *You're letting people down. They think you're not doing a good job. You don't know what you're doing.*

'Have you ever tried to kill yourself?' I did not know, could not say. Panic about not knowing was rising within me. The wording and positioning of the question had a strong, negative impact. It set me back. My reaction was emotional. Resentful. Fearful. But it also led me to realise that although my breakdown had been an episode, a point in time, something in the past, I needed to watch over my reactions in the present and future.

All the questions were written in a forthright style, but that question being last meant it stayed in my mind. Lingered. Ready to be cogitated over. Ripe for rumination. I felt as if all the good work I had done was being pulled away from me. Was I heading towards another breakdown? My husband reminded me of all I had learnt. How far I had come. How much I had overcome. We reviewed my traffic light plan together and he reminded me that my care co-ordinator had explained a recurrence of some signs did not mean another breakdown. It meant it was time to look after myself, using my amber action plan: Challenge my thoughts. Relax. Seek help if necessary.

I went to see my doctor. She reassured me about my reaction and expressed disappointment in the way the form had been constructed. Maybe take any similar forms to her so we could complete them together? She reminded me my psychiatrist had said another breakdown was unlikely and encouraged me to exercise, review my mental health first aid kit and continue doing things I enjoyed. One outcome was our joint decision not to withdraw the anti-depressant tablets. Another was not to try to label that night. Not try to put a name to it. Just accept it had happened.

Another outcome of the discussion with my doctor was to consider a mindfulness course. The university where both my husband and I worked had a positive attitude to wellness, including courses, discounts, and wellness and mental health ambassadors. As mindfulness courses were included in the toolkit available, I opted to enrol. When I began, I learned the clinician facilitating the course was a leader in the mindfulness field. He had published books and articles and ran courses for students, staff and the wider community. I remembered the conversation with my care co-ordinator when I had mentioned mindfulness. What a coincidence to find myself working in the same institution as him.

Our small group met weekly, each session starting with a short mindfulness meditation while the facilitator encouraged us to focus on different parts of the body as we breathed gently. I had always thought there was some great mysticism to meditation: a particular way to sit. A certain frame of mind. Through this practical course I began to understand I could sit in a chair, hands gently in my lap and meditate. The course leader quietly told us to focus on the present, letting go of thoughts and worries. Meanwhile, we carried out a scan of our bodies for tension and stress. He encouraged us to focus on breathing, commenting the breath was always present. The first time he said this, I immediately thought of being snowbound in Scotland. Lying on the living room floor with my mum and sister, panicking over how to breathe correctly. Mum's pithy reply supported the course leader's assertion.

I learned that paying attention to my senses helps focus my mind. Was I thinking too much about something? Replaying a situation again and again? Becoming involved in internal dialogue? I focused on what I was touching. When preparing food, I paid attention to the weight of the knife I was holding. Felt the surface where it met my hand. Noticed how cool it felt to the touch. My mind was occupied with the present.

With the activity. The internal machinations became silent. When I relayed to the group that I tended to worry about things, the course leader said, 'Worry is just worry'. A simple statement. But effective. It made me stop and realise I was wasting energy on something that would not help a situation. Family and friends had told me before that 'there's no point in worrying' but, somehow, I continued to do it. 'Worry is just worry' has stayed with me. I find it to be a powerful, helpful statement.

Talking with group members, I also reflected on how I would think about things I had done or said in the past that I was embarrassed about. Somehow, I could not move past these thoughts. No matter where or when, they seemed to pop into my head. Once there, it was difficult to stop them revolving round and round. The course leader suggested I needed to be more discerning about my thoughts. They would come into my head, but I didn't need to pay attention to them. Instead, focus on breathing, on what I was doing and gently let them go. Discerning. Exactly what I had not been. I had had a dream about driving, where I didn't know how to navigate a junction. Instead of dismissing it, I had allowed it to take over. It had coloured my view of driving and stopped the enjoyment and freedom driving could bring me. As the course leader encouraged us to meditate at the start and end of each day, I resolved to be more discerning in my thoughts. We were also to practise informal mindfulness during the day. This meant paying attention to our surroundings. Listening to sounds around us. Being curious about what we saw. It struck me Mum had commented tearfully, when I was really struggling, that she couldn't imagine not looking up at the sky, seeing the sun, hearing the birds. She practised informal mindfulness, probably without realising it!

I told my husband what I was learning on the course and we discussed whether mindfulness was helping me. I had learned so much at the clinic, but realising I needed to continue to work on my mental health, particularly the way I reacted to situations, led me to want to bolster my personal toolkit. My husband had met the mindfulness course leader and was looking for potential subjects for a massive open online course (MOOC) he was commissioning on the university's behalf with an external provider. Mindfulness seemed to fit the bill. He thought the format of a free online course had the potential to help and impact people across the world. A course was developed, launched and further refined; in three years, over 250,000 people participated. I took part in the first offering. I was keen to find out what online learning was like and found the online learning community to be supportive, helpful and giving of their own experiences. I continued to learn and share with others who, like me, held themselves to higher standards than they would other people. I again recognised how hard I could be on myself, expecting only the best and being frustrated if things did not work out as I hoped.

Do I find mindfulness helpful? It certainly helps my concentration. I notice I focus more on tasks (not just work-related tasks) without my mind thinking about the past or the future. I am also quicker doing things, possibly because I am not being distracted by inconsequential and unrelated thoughts. Although I continue to listen to music while driving, I decided to stop trying to multi-task. I recognised trying to do two different, complex things at once means my attention is switching from one thing to another. I am probably doing neither well. I now give myself permission to complete one before moving to the next.

When attending a resilience workshop organised by my employer, I noticed the impact of mindfulness. The facilitator asked us to look around for thirty seconds, to focus on all the things that were green. Have you tried that? People commented on how many shades of green there were around them. Previously they had viewed them as 'just green'. It was interesting to hear how this simple exercise had shown how much we missed when we didn't pay attention. In another exercise, we were asked to solve ten anagrams. Each showed on a screen for thirty seconds. Meanwhile, the facilitator circled the room clicking a pen, telling us our director had said we were intelligent people. We would have no problem. I noticed how focused I was, not worrying if I couldn't solve one but concentrating on the next as it appeared. Some words didn't have enough vowels if they were in the English language, I thought. At the end, a colleague and I had both solved five of the ten. No one had scored higher. The facilitator's constant pen-clicking had distracted some participants. Others had felt pressure after being unable to solve the first few anagrams and became frustrated. I had noticed the pen-clicking sounds, but I let them wash over me. I didn't spend time worrying as anagrams disappeared from the screen. While this wasn't a scientific experiment, I know my mind tends to flit from one thing to another. I'm sure mindfulness has helped me focus on the here and now.

One thing I learned from my illness was that I didn't have a group of close friends to have fun with, talk to and share things. Not living near my family showed me how important friends were. Developing friendships was one of the key things I resolved to do when we moved. I have discovered, among my group of friends, my 'southern hemisphere twin'. We look nothing alike, but we are similar in so many other ways—even down to our intense fear and dislike of moths! Then there are my two friends who are my parking gurus (and much more!). Despite enjoying driving since my illness, I rarely had to carry passengers. I was so comfortable with these two, happy to admit my driving inadequacies to them and (it has to be said) willing to be the designated driver, their careful instructions have helped me overcome my parallel parking fears. I still celebrate a successful parallel park! And my other friends, of different ages and backgrounds, outlooks and life experiences—each one special to me for their own personal characteristics and the joy we have together.

As well as discovering wonderful friends, I have recognised more about myself. I don't ask for help easily—something I am conscious of and working on. I take things to extremes, whether how long I spend cleaning or the energy I devote to a piece of work. If I see something to be done, my instinct is to do it thoroughly, no half-measures. Now I try to challenge myself to do just enough. And I am a literal person. I stick faithfully to instructions, no deviation from directions and doing things to the letter. This can frustrate my husband, but again, I'm aware of it. To be fair, this helped me get well again. Nonetheless, I try to shake things up now and again, as my counsellor recommended! And I have discovered my happy place, where I feel most at peace and most relaxed—most *me*. The beach. With the sound of waves, sand under my feet and the wind blowing gently, I can lose myself beachcombing: seeing what the tide has brought in. Marvelling at intricate patterns on the sand. Wondering about the journey of things washed up. In awe of my surroundings.

My lovely gran passed away a few years ago. She had chosen to be buried in a cardboard coffin in a woodland cemetery with a crab apple tree planted in her memory. She wanted flowers in spring and apples for the birds in autumn. On my last visit, we counted forty-seven apples. Forty-six on the tree. One fell as we counted!

At the church service after her burial, the minister spoke of Gran wearing a safety pin in her cardigan every day. She thought it was the world's greatest invention and wore it in tribute to Walter Hunt, the American mechanic and inventor who patented it in 1849. We found several newspaper clippings about Walter when we cleared out Gran's cottage, in odd places scattered throughout. The small footprint of her home opened to a myriad of textile and craft gems. We donated her books to the library of the local textile college, since Gran had followed the careers of knitwear and fashion designers who studied there. We offered them handicraft equipment and materials too. The following days found us delivering three knitting machines, five knitting machine tables (we'll never know why there were more tables than machines), a weaving handloom, a table loom, a three-armed loom, shuttles, a spinning wheel, a sewing machine and a milliner's china head. There were bags and bags of wool (including whole fleeces) and bolts of woven material (some from our village mill which closed in the 1960s), which were found in two bedspread-covered chests. Gran lived in a treasure trove. Finding and sorting through her cottage was a wonderful experience for me, Mum and my sister. I returned to Australia with scarves, wraps (with safety pins!), a cashmere dress, jewellery and the little plaque that reads, 'Today's the tomorrow you worried about yesterday and all is well'. I also brought my late grandpa's war-time diaries, small books from the 1940s with pencilled entries. One entry from 27 June 1943 read 'good weather', followed by eight entries recording 'the same'. His diaries were peppered with 'the usual', 'quite a good day' and 'more of the same'. When I read the entry for 9 May 1945 'just the same. War finished today', I realised who I had inherited my poor diary-keeping skills from.

I continue to enjoy baking and cooking. My husband says I look contented and happy when in the kitchen, trying new recipes. I was lucky to spend such a lot of time with Mum when I was ill. I learned not only how to bake, but how to manage a household. Whether buying discounted meat near its sell-by date to freeze, gathering recipes from newspapers and magazines, buying staple items in bulk or having a store cupboard that holds just about everything that could possibly be needed in a kitchen, Mum showed me how to do it. My own store cupboard has grown too. It no longer looks like a student's, and I'm thrilled when I can start straight away on a new recipe without having to go shopping. I've become a fan of bulk-buying and love to score a bargain. My husband admitted his challenge to me when I was ill, to compare prices and buy when products were on offer, was to save money. He thought it would frighten me if he asked me directly, so he thought of fun ways to do it.

When watching one of the *UK Great British Bake-Off* seasons, I was reminded of having something at the forefront of my mind and its potential impact on my actions. Contestants were to make a Sachertorte, a renowned chocolate cake from Vienna. Towards the end of the heat, one female competitor held her piping bag, poised to write Sachertorte on top of her beautiful creation. Simultaneously she talked to the show's comperes, telling them her daughter's name was Sasha. Laughingly, they reminded her to be careful, to write Sachertorte and not her daughter's name. As she piped, Sasha appeared on the cake, without her realising— cue much careful scraping of icing before she tried again. I turned to my husband and reminded him about my psychiatrist's exercise with the farmyard animals and the pyjama-clad hippo.

I have made sure I continue exercising in addition to baking and knitting (blankets, baby items and charity knits). I'm aware how much my body likes exercise. I walk, go to the gym and practise tai chi, which I still love. Besides the different exercises, I have learnt forms or routines including one with a sword. It is particularly graceful (even if I'm not!). I've also enjoyed Zumba and boxing, to shake up my exercise routine a bit (quite literally in the case of Zumba!)

Over the years since I first saw him on breakfast TV and watched *TT3D: Closer to the Edge*, I've continued to look out for Guy Martin, enjoying his television appearances, his turn of phrase, his enthusiasm. I respect how he continues as a lorry mechanic and participates in television programs about his passions—engineering and speed. Most of all, I like that he is his own person. His determination to continue racing, his refusal to submit to fear, despite the crash he had endured, were an inspiration to me.

It has been more than six years since I spoke to the flat-cap man and little boy at the ticket machine. I hope they are doing well. I have thought of them, reflecting that I was regaining my mental freedom at the time he was losing his physical freedom. Both of us different. No idea about the other person. Both of us sharing the experience of limitation. Most of all, I wish I had been able to take the initiative that day, to ask the man for his girlfriend's telephone number so I could tell her we had spoken. To ask her to spend the rest of the day with him. As I have gained so much from my experience, I hope he has had a similar positive experience—that he is looking forward, not back. Just as others had hope for me, I have hope for him.

In the months after my illness, I joked with my husband that I would write about all that had happened. When we talked about it, it seemed less of a joke and more of a good idea. I had felt so scared. So alone. Since I didn't know anyone who had experienced something similar, I thought nothing like it could have happened to anyone else. I longed to be able to look at someone's face and know that they had had a breakdown and survived. I longed to be encouraged by someone who had gone through it and come out the other side. I longed to be reassured by someone who knew—because I didn't. So even though mental health is talked about more openly now than ten years ago, I am adding my name and my face to this story in the hope that it helps someone else who doesn't know.

I kept everything related to my breakdown and recovery: the stick-man drawings to my husband, the official letters from work, my care plan, my traffic light plan, my little black book with handwritten recipes, my drawings from art therapy classes, my depression cape, my medical notes, the letters from therapists and doctors, the card with 'The Rules of Assertion', my stories from the creative writing classes, my Edward Hedgehog diaries where I wrote all my appointments, the tatting shuttles, my notes from the anxiety management course, the relaxation CD with the voice of the gently spoken, paper-shuffling woman, and cards and letters from friends. All of it. Looking through, I was struck by the notes I prepared for my first meeting with the psychiatrist. They are written in capital letters, maybe to emphasise how I felt? It seems incredible that I managed to draw these thoughts together, to put them down on paper, when I was struggling so badly. Months after I had written my mantra, I realised I had inadvertently used the surname of my general practitioner for my counsellor too. Funny to think I had looked at those words so often and not noticed, not realised I had given two people with different surnames the same one. I still have that piece of paper too. A tattered, torn, tangible reminder of the reassurance I craved.

Going through all this material to tell my story has been fun. It has been challenging. At times, heart-wrenching. Some things only now make sense. Looking at my drawing of boxes with nine squares, some of them coloured in, connected to each other apart from one box, I realised that box was me. Despite being with the others, it was solitary. On the outside looking in. When I drew it, I knew that box belonged on its own, but I didn't understand why. Why was it unconnected? What made me draw it that way? Only now do I realise I was reflecting how I felt: Alone. On the edge. Marginalised.

The most surprising thing about writing about my experience is that I have truly felt the pain of my situation. I didn't feel it at the time. I didn't feel anything. Writing about Mum as she broke down in tears, peeling carrots in the kitchen, telling me through sobs that she couldn't stop me harming myself, left me doubled over in pain. I felt as if my heart was being ripped out my chest. That was so hard to recall. The beauty of the sky outside and Mum's tear-stained face, as she tried to deal with a situation that neither of us had predicted. It hurt so, so much to think about the pain and helplessness she must have been feeling.

Writing my story has helped me come to terms with my breakdown. I found it hard to accept that isolation at work, the potential impact of financial cuts and the pressure I felt could cause such distress. Add in high personal standards, a negative and ruminative way of thinking, a poor work–life balance, a fear of driving, the missing network of close friends and the lack of exercise, and it's no wonder I couldn't cope anymore. I have been asked what triggered my breakdown, but I don't think there was one particular trigger. I think it was a combination—a slow-burn effect and I was worn down.

Have there been any lasting effects from my breakdown? I am no longer confident with arithmetic. I used to be able to add up the prices of items I was buying. Now, I try, but it takes me longer and my addition is more of a guesstimate. I also find it difficult to copy down numbers when they are told to me. I double-check telephone and reference numbers. I find it hard to listen to the numbers and write them down simultaneously. Often the order is incorrect, two numbers transposed. These are not serious or bad things, but they are obvious to me. However, I'm aware of them and have worked out a way to overcome mistakes.

I also continue to take medication. If someone had told me I would still take a tablet daily after all these years, I would have rebelled against taking medication even more than I did. Although my doctor and I reduced and then removed the anti-psychotic medication, I remained on the anti-depressant medication. At first, I viewed this as failure. I equated being well with being medication-free. A wise friend helped me see otherwise. She said some people needed medication to enable them to play on a level playing-field. And I am happy to play on this field. It works for me.

People have asked me how I got better. How did I go from being very seriously ill, unable to do anything other than feed and clothe myself, having to be led from room to room by Mum and told what to do, to being independent, returning to work and functioning normally again?

I think there were different things that helped me get better. I really wanted to be well again. I was prepared to do whatever was necessary to help myself. I think I recognised the medical professionals would help me, but it was down to me to help myself too. They could not do it for me. Whether this was taking medication, participating in the anxiety management course, undertaking CBT, I feel I tried my best. I listened to the psychiatrists, doctors, nurses, counsellors and occupational therapists and followed their advice. In the early stages I couldn't work out when to take medication, so it had to be given to me. After that, I made sure I knew what medication to take, how much and when to take it. And I followed instructions (I know, not a difficult thing for me to do!). There seemed to be so much chance around getting the right medication and dosage, I didn't want to do anything to jeopardise my recovery. Or delay it. The doctors told me when to take the tablets and I took them. They said not to take alcohol with them, so I didn't. I wanted them to see me and how I was progressing (or otherwise). Failing to take medication or obscuring its effect with alcohol wouldn't help them to help me. So, I think my commitment to recovery and my determination were critical. It was hard work. Don't let anyone tell you any different. Until you are seriously ill, I don't think you can understand how much effort it takes to recover. It becomes your full-time job. Your focus. Your everything.

I didn't know what was happening to me. And I didn't know what it would take for me to get better. It took a lot of resources and a lot of people to put me on the road to recovery, to help me identify what had led up to my breakdown and how to look after myself in future. It took resources and people, doing what they know best, to make me independent again and a member of the workforce. Until it happened to me and I lived through it, I couldn't have imagined what a seriously mentally ill person would need. Did I need support in a time of crisis? Yes, I needed it and my family needed it too. Did I need specialist support? Yes, I did. The psychiatrist diagnosed my illness, prescribed the right medication and, by challenging me and my thoughts, helped me find freedom. Did I need general practitioner support? Yes, I did. My general practitioner knew me when I was well, was able to access the help I needed, monitored my progress and continued to oversee my care. Did I need therapy? Yes, the therapists worked with me to identify my problems of perfectionism, my negative thoughts and my ruminative style of thinking. Did I need occupational therapy support? Yes, I did. The long days I had to endure while I was unable to motivate myself or direct my own time exacerbated my situation. I needed someone to give my day structure and activities to fill it. Did I need drivers to take me to appointments? Yes, I needed someone to transport me. More than that, I needed contact with the outside world and the drivers provided that. Did I need employment support? Yes, I did. The world of work seemed daunting. The necessary formal nature of communications with my employer forbidding. I needed someone beside me at meetings, to ask questions on my behalf if I could not and to give me confidence. Did I need the support of pharmacists, nurses, receptionists and community services? Yes, they all played a vital part in the operation. They explained things to me. Reassured me. Treated me with kindness.

It took all these resources and all these people. And I didn't pay directly for any of it, as I was treated on the National Health Service. When I could not earn money, when I thought we might lose our home and when I ate scraps for lunch, how could I have paid for it? So, when there are calls for money to be saved on our health services, I reflect on my experience. When priorities need to be determined, I see the faces of the people who gave me a second chance at life.

Everyone who was involved in my recovery—all the medical staff, doctors, psychiatrists, therapists, support staff, nurses, drivers, pharmacists and receptionists—showed me nothing but love, care and respect. Someone they didn't know, had never met, had never crossed paths with before. Me. A stranger. They went out of their way to help me, support me and teach me how to get better. They did all this with love, care and respect. Did I treat strangers that way? Can you say you treat strangers that way? Are we gentle in our words, kind in our actions and thoughtful in the way we treat each other? How much better it could be if we all chose to emulate those people who offer love, care and respect to strangers they meet.

Not only did I have the help and support of wonderful medical services, I had the most fantastic neighbours, who included me in their daily life without hesitation. My neighbour told me we would get through this. She was right.

I was lucky, too, in having the most wonderful support network in my parents and sister. They cajoled me, encouraged me, kept me occupied. They did what they do naturally. They loved. And laughed.

And my husband, who held me when words had no meaning, reassured me when I questioned whether I would get better and demonstrated his love for me in the most difficult of situations. All in his quiet, patient way. He brought joy and laughter back to my life and his positivity inspired me. He has my love forever.

My nervous breakdown was hideous. Frightening. Like something I never dreamed could happen. Something I wouldn't change for the world. I learnt so much during and from it. I learnt how it feels to be marginalised and vulnerable, how to accept advocacy and support, and how to recognise when I'm well and what to do when I'm not. I met some wonderful people who genuinely helped and inspired me, whether they realised it or not. And I got to know me again—the Imperfect, Perfect, Ali Plus.

NOTES

1. C Williams. *Overcoming Depression and Low Mood: A Five Areas Approach* (London: Arnold, 2001)
2. Morecambe, Eric & Wise, Ernie. *"Positive Thinking."* Morecambe *& Wise – Songs and Sketches,* composed by Tony Hatch and Jackie Trent, Universal Music Publishing Group, 1971. If you have never heard of, or watched, Morecambe & Wise, I recommend them!
3. *The Traffic Light* Pack was an internal clinic resource designed by H Hook, OT and R North, CPN. (2008).
4. D Keable. *The Management of Anxiety* (New York: Churchill Livingstone, 1997).
5. L Mitchell. *Simple Relaxation* (London: John Murray, 1977).
6. H Benson. *The Relaxation Response* (New York: Collins, 1976).

Acknowledgements

A big thank you to Andy McDermott of Publicious Book Publishing Services for helping bring this dream to fruition and sharing his knowledge and experience of publishing. As my story is very personal, it was one that I was keen to tell myself and in my own way and Andy has enabled me to do just that. Thank you also to Patricia Kot, who assessed my first draft manuscript (it was way too long) and edited later versions. She provided helpful comments, challenges and suggestions, was my grammar guru and, most importantly, maintained my voice.

I don't know how to express my thanks to all those who were involved in my care. I remember them with respect, fondness and gratitude and hope this book serves as a tribute to their dedication and the important work that they do.

To Jenny, Garry, Walter and Donna (who also provided the beach shot on the back cover), thank you from the bottom of my heart. Talking to you about my experience, your questions and our conversations have helped shape this book. Thank you too, to friends who encouraged me to continue with *Knitting, Tatting and Nervous Breakdowns* (when it may have seemed unlikely that anything would be produced!) - Kim, Sandra, Maureen, Cathryn, Dianne, Rick, Cedric, Deb, Christine, Matthew, Bernie, Eliza and Louisa.

To Beryl and Brian, who were beyond neighbourly. Who cared for me like one of their own family. Lots of love to you both, I miss our kitchen table chats!

To my sister, Lisa, who has shown me what true determination really is. I love you, cookie.

To my Mum and Dad – Jennifer and Bill. My registration colleagues used to talk about parents giving their children "roots and wings". You are the epitome of those parents. I love you.

And to Darrell, my positive-thinking confidant, who cherished my stick-drawing letters and continues to cherish me. Just as I cherish you. All my love xx.

Appendix 1: My Top Tips

Over time, I have found these things work best for me:

- *The Contrast Muscle Relaxation* If I'm anxious or over-tired, the practice of tensing and then releasing the muscles around my body helps remind me of the lovely feel of warm, loose muscles compared to the tight, taut, rigid ones I had before.

- *Focusing on my senses* I find focusing on my sense of touch to be very helpful. Concentrating on the feel of something in my hand or where my feet connect to the ground can shift my mind away from troubling or repetitive thoughts.

- *The Relaxation Response* When I find it hard to get to sleep, I use this mental tension control technique. I've found that relaxing my body, focusing on breathing in and out, and saying the word 'one' to myself has been much more successful then counting sheep!

- *Reminding myself that anxiety is normal and I can manage it* It's important for me to remember that I will feel anxious and uncertain at times…and this is normal!

Why not find out what works for you?

Appendix 2: *Knitting, Tatting and Nervous Breakdowns recipe book*

Shortbread
The rice flour adds some crunch and the corn flour some silkiness

12 oz butter
6 oz caster sugar
12 oz plain flour
3 oz rice flour (or semolina)
3 oz corn flour

Pre-heat oven to 170°. Beat butter and sugar together until soft and smooth, then add flour, rice flour and corn flour. Mix then use hand to gather into a ball. Press into a sandwich tin, spread the mixture evenly and prick with a fork. On the long edge, use a fork handle to make fantails.

Put in oven for 40 minutes until golden brown (cover with baking paper after 30 minutes if necessary). Remove from oven and replace with second empty sandwich tin. Shake over caster sugar, cut down the middle and then cut slices across. Remove warmed second tray and switch off oven. Take slices from the first tray and arrange both trays so that slices sit like a zip – with room between them. Allow to dry and cool. Enjoy!

Mum's oatcakes
I love eating them with hard cheddar cheese and an apple, but they're perfect on their own

8 oz self-raising flour
1 tsp bicarbonate of soda
½ tsp salt

1 lb pinhead oatmeal (course Scottish oats – in Australia they're called steel-cut oats)
5 oz butter
3 fl oz each full cream milk and water mixed together

Pre-heat oven to 165°. Sift flour, soda and salt into a bowl. Stir in the oatmeal and mix. Rub in butter thoroughly, then add the milk and water mixture. Sieve flour on a surface, divide mixture in two and roll out dough (which will be quite wet, don't worry about using lots of flour!). Use a scone cutter to make rounds (about 2 inches / 5 cm in diameter). Bake until pale golden for a minimum of 20 – 30 minutes. (I tend to remove after 20 minutes, turn off the oven and when cooler, put them back in). Store in an airtight container.

Dad's carrot and lentil soup

A hearty lunchtime favourite

Olive oil
Slice of butter
3 – 4 onions, chopped
3 – 4 carrots, chopped
Tablespoon of bouillon
½ pound of washed lentils
Boiling water
Sugar
Salt and pepper

Sweat onions and carrots in butter and oil. Add bouillon and stir. Add lentils and then hot water.
Bring to pressure, when main weight is fizzing steadily, reduce heat and cook for 10 minutes. Remove from heat. Once pressure has dropped, open pressure cooker, add a teaspoon of sugar, salt and pepper and mash soup.

Savoury bread and butter pudding

Great for using up left-over bread and when you can't access the freezer!

Bacon, chopped
Onion, chopped
Cheese, grated
Bread
2 eggs
Milk (less than half a pint)

Preheat oven to 170°C. Butter a casserole dish. Fry off bacon and onion. Layer bread, bacon and onion, cheese and then repeat. Pour over egg and milk mixture, add a final layer of cheese and then bake for 45 minutes.

Fish Pie

A filling meal with few ingredients. Just remember to cook accompanying vegetables!

2 fish fillets (haddock, river cobbler or barramundi, deboned if necessary)
White sauce (I now use 3 oz butter, 3 oz plain flour, 1½ pints milk, salt and pepper)
Tomato, skinned and sliced
Cheese, sliced
Mashed potatoes

Preheat oven to 190°C. Butter a casserole dish. Make the white sauce by melting butter, adding flour then stirring for one minute. Remove from the heat and gradually stir in milk, before bringing to the boil and stirring to thicken. Pour half the white sauce into the dish. Lay the fish on top. Put remainder of white sauce on fish. Add a layer of tomatoes followed by a layer of cheese. Top with mashed potatoes and bake for 30 minutes.

Lightning Source UK Ltd.
Milton Keynes UK
UKHW011159071220
374767UK00006B/952

9 780648 946502